THE SURVIVOR'S LEGACY

How the Holocaust Shaped Future
Generations

The Survivor's Legacy:
How the Holocaust Shaped Future Generations

By
Sally Lefton Wolfe
and
Michael Leonard Farkas

with
Margery Walshaw

Contents

Author's Note

Although the Holocaust occurred 75 years prior to this writing, the aftermath and its toll on survivors and their families still plagues us today. This book combines history, studies, and personal stories. In many places, names have been changed at the request of individuals who to this day, find it beyond difficult to speak of the horrors of war.

Preface

WHY A HYPHEN MATTERS —

It may seem like a simple choice — to hyphenate or not. However, the proper printed form of the word "anti-semitism" was debated carefully among scholars and religious leaders, and ultimately, the International Holocaust Remembrance Alliance (IHRA) addressed it for the world.

The reason for all of the discussion and debate? The goal: to ultimately eradicate violence, hatred, and any mistreatment toward Jews. So how does a small hyphen fit into this discussion?

The term antisemitism is often printed as 'anti-Semitism' with a hyphen. Even Microsoft's auto-correct feature makes this suggestion. The concern is that the hyphenated spelling legitimizes "Semitism" and allows a racial classification associated with Nazi ideology. Furthermore, by dividing the term, it strips away its meaning of opposition and hatred toward Jews.

To bring a historical context to this subject, the philological term 'Semitic' referred to a body of languages originating in the Middle East. Following this history, adding the prefix 'anti' with 'Semitism' indicates antisemitism to those who speak Semitic languages or are classified as 'Semites'. But in more recent history, the term has referred to prejudice against Jews.

The modern term gained popularity in Germany and Europe at the time of the Enlightenment in Europe, and a pseudo-scientific racial theory created within Nazi ideology during the twentieth century.

The Enlightenment's emancipation laws led Jews to assimilate into non-Jewish, German-speaking society. Mass conversions to Christianity occurred along with the emergence of Reform Judaism in the 1840s. More traditional Jewish observances lost their importance and were in fact, criticized. This criticism wasn't only against Judaism as a religion, but also as an ethnicity.

Whether Jews could be regarded as Germans became a point of discussion. Many argued that because Semitic languages had a history originating in the Middle East and spoken across Western Asia and North Africa that Jews were "different" and an "Oriental" people. This theory was popularized by a prominent historian, Heinrich von Treitschke.

Many who expressed hatred toward the Jews came up with the concept of Jewish "otherness" and was coined as "semitism." According to an essay by the International Holocaust Remembrance Alliance, "To express their own rejection of this "semitism," German Jew-haters started to call themselves adherents of the ideology of "antisemitism" (Antisemitismus) and themselves "antisemites" (Antisemiten). It was most notably the journalist Wilhelm Marr who popularized the word. Marr even founded the

"League of Antisemites" (Antisemitenliga), the first German organization committed to fighting the alleged Jewish power taking over Germany."

Soon, other politicians followed Marr's agenda. It's interesting to note that the anti-Jewish propaganda started long before Hitler. An organizer of the antisemitic political movement was Otto Böckel, who ran for election in 1887 as a Reichstag (parliamentary) candidate on a "independent antisemite" platform. He was elected and three years later, officially established the Antisemitic People's Party (Antisemitische Volkspartei).

By writing "antisemitism" with a hyphen, we inadvertently accept the falseness that Treitschke, Marr, and Böckel proposed — that (Western) Jews are essentially "other". A "Semitic ethnicity" or a "Semitic people" does not exist. There is only a Semitic language of which Hebrew belongs, along with Arabic, Syriac, Amharic and others.

During these times of negative rhetoric toward Jews and increased violence, it should be clear that antisemitism is a modern term for Jew hatred. Education about the non-hyphenated term is supported and launched by The International Holocaust Remembrance Alliance (IHRA), an intergovernmental body whose purpose is to place political and social leaders' support behind the need for Holocaust education, remembrance, and research both nationally and internationally.

Words are powerful and have influence. Words create a written history. Therefore, scholars and Jewish activists recommend not hyphenating the word to dispel the notion of an entity called "Semitism," which "anti-Semitism" opposes. With an increase in hate crimes, this clarity is of utmost importance.

Introduction

> **We must always take sides.
> Neutrality helps the oppressor,
> never the victim. Silence
> encourages the tormentor, never the
> tormented.**
>
> **The opposite of love is not hate,
> it's indifference.**
>
> **There may be times when we are
> powerless to prevent injustice, but
> there must never be a time when we
> fail to protest.** — *Elie Wiesel*

At the time that this book was launched in 2020, an unprecedented protest was underway. It began with a hashtag in 2013, grew to new levels with the shooting deaths of three innocents at the hands of authorities in the United States, and transcended into a worldwide, human rights movement.

When Elie Wiesel wrote in 1958 (1960 in English

translation) his warning about failure to protest, he demonstrated his foresight. His book, *Night*, is a sparse, but gripping account of his experience, alongside his father, in the concentration camps at Auschwitz and Buchenwald in 1944-1945.

Wiesel's father didn't survive the camps. He was just three months shy of being liberated by the 6th Armored Division of the United States Army. When his father died, Elie couldn't have known that liberation was imminent or that he would survive. Yet, certainly he would have recognized that if survival was in his future, his past experiences would always remain.

And so it is with other survivors, whether of the Holocaust or a different human rights injustice. Our experiences shape our future, and with protests and writings, we create history that is shared and experienced, for better or worse, by our descendants.

This is the objective of this book and its first-hand stories — to create an account of the effects of the Holocaust on the descendants of its survivors.

Wiesel, who took on the role of caretaker for his father, wrote of his experience, "Here there are no fathers, no brothers, no friends." His account was originally written in Yiddish and first published in Argentina. With help from another author, François Mauriac, Wiesel's words were translated and published in French, and two years later, published once again in English by Hill & Wang.

This circuitous route of publishing is reminiscent of

Wiesel's own fortitude and that of so many other Jews, both those who perished as well as those who survived. Literary critic Ruth Franklin described the transformation of *Night* from Yiddish into French as an "angry historical account into a work of art." It is with understanding that the words are angry. Why should they not be? Who could leave such an experience unscathed?

If Wiesel's words were originally "angry" it is indicative of the emotion that poured from the souls of countless others. Yet, most remained silent or were silenced. Those who survived may not have told their tales to the world, but their descendants always knew that they bore the label of "survivor."

Jews who lived through the Holocaust share terrible and similar histories. Unlike them, their descendants have varying life experiences. Some heard detailed accounts of their parents' suffering and survival. Others were told next to nothing about the war. Those who learned first-hand accounts were often raised with fear. One might imagine that the descendants who were spared the gruesome tales grew up without any negative ramifications. Yet, growing up in an idyllic reality is to live in a false reality. Neither the children of the survivors who provided details of the Holocaust or those whose parents kept secrets were spared from their own personal suffering.

The research and interviews that went into creating this book revealed descendants of Holocaust survivors suffering a myriad of emotional ailments. From PTSD (post traumatic stress disorder) to initiating abuse against their spouses and children, denial, eating and feeding disorders, and avoidance.

This book will explore what it means to be a descendant of a Holocaust survivor. Important questions will be asked and explored including:

- Will there come a time to let go of the past and put the phrase "never forget" to rest?
- If so, how does a Jew today convey their history while still being a good parent, a loving spouse, and a well-adjusted individual?
- In their determination to remember a troubling history have Holocaust survivors shaped subsequent generations for better or worse?

To answer these questions, numerous first-hand interviews were conducted, online research was collected, and personal stories were shared. Some of the facts are heart-wrenching; others are heart-warming. No history is complete without attention to both sides.

Chapter 1

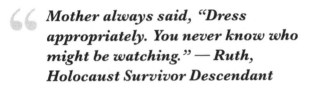 **Mother always said, "Dress appropriately. You never know who might be watching." — Ruth, Holocaust Survivor Descendant**

I magine growing up with the notion of being watched. Like a museum exhibit, a caged animal, or in Ruth's case, the woman who retold the quote above, a Jew. The idea of being watched can be disconcerting to anyone, but if that concept is told to a child, who then grows up believing that unseen forces are watching and lurking, the effects can be debilitating.

Such is the fate that befell Ruth whose parents' experiences in the Holocaust shaped her own perception of reality.

"I always felt the need to look over my shoulder. My behavior mirrored my mother's, which was shaped by the war."

Ruth admits that her fear of danger lurking influenced how she acted as a teenager. Rather than be carefree and untroubled, she was filled with a sense of responsibility and even anger.

THE HOLOCAUST — THE WORLD WAR II GENOCIDE OF European Jews from 1942 to 1945 — claimed six million Jewish lives who were imprisoned in concentration camps. Under Hitler's control, German occupied Europe designed a systematic method for eliminating anyone who followed Jewish tradition and religion, or was simply of Jewish descent no matter how far removed.

The Holocaust wiped out two-thirds of Europe's Jewish population. The survivors may have made it out of the concentration camps, escaping gas chambers, mass shootings, live burials, or the grueling work and lack of food that also claimed lives, but they didn't leave the war unscathed.

It is now 75 years after the liberation of Auschwitz, the most well-known of the Nazi death camps. Its infamy is due to it being the largest of the camps, the fact that over one million Jews lost their lives at that one location, and that its sole purpose was to kill Jews and other "undesirables." The concentration camps had one slight difference; they were also used for detainment and labor.

In a January 25, 2020 article from *The Economist* magazine, it states, "The tally of the dead is hard to comprehend. Of the 9.5 million Jews in Europe before the war, 6 million were murdered. If you spent five minutes reading about each of them, it would fill every waking hour for 90 years."

A museum in Israel, known as Yad Vashem ("A Memorial and a Name"), is working to document and commemorate every Holocaust victim. With six million Jews killed, it's a monumental task originally conceived by Sarah Friedlander, a survivor of Bergen-Belsen and the first director of this archive.

Since Yad Vashem's documentation began in 2004, its database has grown from 2.7 million people to 4.8 million. The entries attempt to memorialize the victims with biographies, links to other relatives, and any other information that survivors can provide. This growing historical account is impressive, but with nearly 2 million more people to be found, there is still a lot of work to be done. Yad Vashem believes that today 400,000 Jews who survived or fled the Nazis are alive. Within ten years, that number could be fewer than 100,000 surviving Jews.

※

YOUTH WITH ADULT RESPONSIBILITIES

When Ruth was around ten-years-old, she recalls feeling angry that her friends would talk about visiting their grandparents' homes, but she never did.

"I knew something had happened that caused me not to have grandparents, let alone ever meet them. However, the reason for this was a secret because neither my mother, nor my father, ever spoke about the Holocaust."

Yet, although her parents didn't speak about their time in the Holocaust, the memories of that period stayed with them and resulted in a parenting style that was both strict and protective. "I had slightly more freedom with my father than my mother. Perhaps, it was because I worked in the family business alongside him."

The family business was a coffee shop in Los Angeles where Ruth worked every day after school as well as weekends. Ruth recognized that going off to work each day made her different from her school friends. But the differences didn't end there. Most of her friends' parents were born in the United States. Ruth noted that her family maintained an unspoken language — one that she recognized as an understanding of what it meant to be Jewish — as well as a language unique from her school friends. "My parents spoke to me in Yiddish. I not only understood it, but could also speak it back."

She recalls pressure by her parents to help in their business, while also maintaining good grades and succeeding in school. In order to comply, they instilled many boundaries. "I wasn't allowed to go out as much as my siblings," Ruth recalls. She surmises that by the time her siblings were born and reached an age of maturity, her parents had relaxed a bit in their fears and views.

"My siblings were allowed to get cars, but I wasn't although I had the money to buy one," notes Ruth. "I was told that a car would give me too much freedom." In her parents' minds, the price of freedom was her safety. They wanted Ruth either at school, at work, or at home.

Even though her parents began to lessen their control with her siblings because nothing terrible had occurred to Ruth, the affect of their fear and previous control had already permeated Ruth's core. The damage had settled, still brewing below the surface.

PSYCHOLOGICAL SYMPTOMS IN CHILDREN OF HOLOCAUST SURVIVORS

Rita's mom was born in Hungary and her father was from Greece. She describes her childhood as living in a constant state of chaos and confusion with her mother and siblings living in fear of her father's next outburst. They never knew if he was going to hug or hit them.

As a result, Rita's mother was extremely possessive and never wanted her to leave the house or even have friends. Her mother also told her devastating stories from her experience in the Holocaust. Rita became her mother's emotional caregiver, but the burden was too much for her and Rita suffered a breakdown.

Her mother took her to a psychiatrist who prescribed tranquilizers. She recalls that her life felt as if she lived in a fog. Her sister married when she was just 12, making her mother even more possessive of Rita.

When Rita was planning her own wedding at the age of 18, her mother told her that she planned to leave her father when Rita married. The guilt was too much, and Rita suffered even further mental trauma coupled with agoraphobia. She began taking anti-depressants.

Later in life, Rita was asked if her father was an alcoholic because his behavior was similar to one. Rita's own therapist referred to him as a dry alcoholic. But her mom insisted that nobody could reveal his behavior. She wanted the rest of the world to believe they had the perfect family even though he hit all of them regularly. And because she would try to defy him, Rita became his favorite target.

Her mother died in 1989. Yet just six months after her death, Rita's therapist said she didn't need therapy anymore. Looking back, Rita believes that there was nothing that could be described as normal regarding her childhood and teen years.

Today is much different. She is now 65 and happy with grown children and grandchildren to love.

Like Rita and her sister, Ruth married at a young age. She was just shy of 20-years-old. Looking back at her marriage, she believes that committing to a relationship at a young age was more about getting out of the house than about feeling in love. It wasn't until her early 30s when the fear of being watched fully developed in her mind, and ironically, what she most wanted — her freedom — was what she now feared. Ruth began to feel uncomfortable with the very idea of leaving the house.

Initially, this feeling of being uncomfortable was limited to specific situations. The 1971 San Fernando earthquake (also known as the Sylmar earthquake) rocked Los Angeles where Ruth was then living. It jolted her psyche making her fear being trapped inside a collapsed building. She began to avoid incidents that would trigger severe mental discomfort.

If ever she was in a car and had to enter a tunnel, she would close her eyes and wish for the other side to appear soon. She had a growing concern about her safety when leaving the house, but attempted to push the fear away for the sake of her marriage.

She started to explore her feelings and with this new, inward journey, she also asked her parents about the Holocaust. "I became more aware of the Holocaust once I was married because I saw television shows about it," says Ruth.

However, even though she asked questions, she didn't receive many answers. "My mother would simply change the subject. My father spoke more openly to me, but only when we were at work."

After her father passed away, Ruth began to feel like a

substitute for him in her mother's eyes. To remove pressure from her mother, Ruth handled the business affairs. This independence ended, however, in 1983.

Her youngest daughter was two-and-a-half-years-old. Fears of being crushed by toppling buildings consumed Ruth. An inability to leave the house presented itself on frequent occasions. One day, her husband took her to a doctor and she was given medication to help her relax. The result was a panic attack more severe than any she had experienced.

She assumed it was an allergic reaction to the medication. Her husband attempted to get her to another doctor, but when it came time to leave, she simply couldn't walk out the door. Six months went by and like the realization of her problem that happened after the earthquake, another new awareness erupted.

Ruth was watching a television show about agoraphobia and realized the symptoms matched her own. Finally, she felt she had answers. There was a name for what plagued her, and she thought she could find answers and solutions. She tried relaxation tapes; however, she found little success with this technique. At the same time, she started to have problems with her father-in-law who was unsupportive and even dismissive of her condition.

Ruth recalls going out to dinner with the family. "It was difficult, but made even worse by my father-in-law who would exclude me from any conversation." At one point, her children posed a suggestion: they and Ruth could sit at one table and their father could sit at another with his parents. "It was like being married to two men," Ruth notes of life with her husband and father-in-law.

It's difficult to determine which issue created the root problems for Ruth. Her own parents' refusal to speak of the Holocaust, yet instilling a fear of being watched encouraged Ruth's desire to stay home, away from unwanted attention. The 1971 earthquake contributed to her fear of being away from home should she become trapped in a collapsing structure. Her resulting agora-phobia perhaps gave her reason to distance further from her husband and his family. Whether the agoraphobia perpetuated her marriage's demise or allowed her to leave it is unknown even in Ruth's mind.

She stayed in her marriage for 25 years. She has explored these questions and more with numerous thera-pists. Over the years, she has experienced times of remission when she can function at a certain level and be away from home. Four years ago, a sickness left her wheelchair bound and today, she prefers to be at home.

LIKE RUTH, KAREN HAD MANY RESPONSIBILITIES growing up. But in contrast, as an adult she maintains a multitude of responsibilities in her successful career as a real estate broker. Her adult success may be attributed to being raised never to complain. If she ever wavered from this mandate, her mother would say, "Don't you dare complain. You're lucky to have food. I had to sneak out to get a potato." But Karen didn't fully understand her moth-er's words.

Her mother was only five-years-old when the war began. She saw her own mother being led to the gas cham-ber, and also lost her father and brother. Her aunt and uncle took her in, but life was difficult. They survived by hiding in a cave and the aftermath affected Karen's mother for the rest of her life. She had no control over her life as a child, so she developed the need to control everything around her as an adult.

Karen had trouble accepting her mother's ways. Everything worked on a schedule. Monday was designated for doing laundry; Tuesday was groceries; Wednesday was dusting, and so on. Wanting to get away, Karen hid in the backyard. When her mother found her, she was furious. It was then, when Karen was 13-years-old, that she learned her mother was a Holocaust survivor and her entire family was killed.

Her mother said, "How dare you run away. You should be grateful you have a home." Karen's reaction was to become rebellious. She started partying to break away from her mother's control. At age 16, she graduated from high school and moved out.

After many years of therapy, Karen and her mother dramatically improved their relationship.

※

SIMILARLY, DONNA IS A SUCCESSFUL businesswoman from Agoura Hills, California. Her parents came from Greece, and her mother was one of nine children. Sadly, her mother was the only sibling to survive the Holocaust.

On the day of liberation, her mother had been placed in a concentration camp hospital where the Nazis planned to conduct medical experiments on her. Luckily, she was freed before more damage could be inflicted on her.

Donna's father also miraculously escaped from the work camp where he was sent. A kind, Christian family hid him and changed his name. After the war, both parents returned to Greece, later met and married. Donna was born in Greece, but soon after, moved to the United States where her four siblings were born.

In spite of growing up in the U.S. long after the war ended, Donna grew up in a shroud of fear. Whenever she left the house, her mother suffered anxiety attacks until her return. Although he had little education, Donna's father ran a successful business. His awareness of the tragedy he overcame resulted in developing a demanding demeanor. He was particularly hard on Donna's mother and herself since she was the eldest sibling, sometimes inflicting physical abuse.

Expectations came easily from her parents; encouragement did not. Donna fretted about what the neighbors thought of them. One day she and her parents were in the car and her father began hitting her mother without provocation. Her mother jumped from the car to the witness of neighbors. Donna was mortified.

Wanting to avoid speculation, Donna kept to herself and grew more shy and wary of outsiders. Life in and outside of the home was stressful. When the subject of the Holocaust arose on television, her mother would cry. The knowledge of her parents' past plagued Donna and she felt guilty if she sought or experienced enjoyment. On rare occasions, she snuck out to parties, but never had fun due to guilt.

Prior to marrying, her mother worked in retail, but left her job in favor of becoming a housewife. Donna's father had a controlling nature and as a result, forbid her mother from learning to drive. Similarly, her parents agreed that Donna should focus her efforts on finding a husband. In spite of becoming a workaholic to avoid this plan, Donna wed at age 20, marrying the first man she ever dated simply to escape her family.

Yet, when she reflects about her mother's acquiescence toward her father, Donna realizes she tried her best. Later in life, her parents' relationship improved. They passed away within a year of each other — in 2001 and 2002, respectively.

Donna has found perspective regarding her parents, acknowledging that one cannot endure the trauma they experienced unscathed. Her parents came to the United States with nothing, but created a successful business and a family encompassing six children, 14 grandchildren and 17 great-grandchildren. Pre-Covid, Donna and her extended family held a large get-together to focus on living their best lives and to honor their parents.

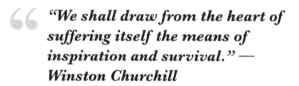

Chapter 2

"We shall draw from the heart of suffering itself the means of inspiration and survival." — *Winston Churchill*

Ruth cites the 1971 Sylmar earthquake as one of the catalysts for her debilitating agoraphobia. Yet, there is no doubt in her mind and those of her siblings, Lenny and Sally, that being a child of a Holocaust survivor was also a root cause of her illness.

The Holocaust survivors' legacy is vast. As Sally and Lenny will attest, in their family it hasn't just affected first generation children, but second generations as well. Lenny's two daughters, Tammy and Samantha, became a source of comfort for their grandmother, who suffered from nightmares for most of her life after the Holocaust.

While her husband was alive, the children continued to be sheltered from her episodes, but when her husband passed away, she couldn't sleep alone. They had rented the top floor of their duplex out to another family, but upon her husband's passing, they evicted the family so that Lenny's family could be closer — so close that grand-daughters Tammy and Samantha could take over in sleeping with their grandmother to prevent her nightmares.

"Although Tammy helped, the responsibility mainly fell with Samantha who would go downstairs to sleep with my mother," says Lenny. Samantha was five-years-old when this habit started and at the time, she was happy to have sleep-overs with grandma and be of help. When she became a teenager, however, there was some resent-ment over having to take on this role, but still she accepted her grandmother's debilitating condition and helped until her 20s when her grandmother passed away.

Sally notes that her mother's nightmares inadver-tently affected her niece's sleep patterns. Agoraphobia afflicted her sister, Ruth. And, many other members of her family experienced forms of anxiety including herself, her brother Lenny, and her son. Their research into the subject shows that the manner in which this type of anxiety manifests is very different from person to person.

As the youngest sibling, Sally believes she was shel-tered from much of her parents' history during the Holo-caust. As Ruth explained, initially their parents refused to talk about the Holocaust. The silence was originally enforced by their mother, but as Ruth's desire for knowl-edge about the war persisted, eventually their parents discussed their experience. Sally, however, blocked out many of the stories, either because they were too terrible or she was simply too young to comprehend that these atrocities could happen to her own parents.

"It could have been a defense mechanism on my part," explains Sally. "And yet, my own son also has experienced anxiety." Her son, Ryan, lost his father at age 16. Although not a child, the teenage years are formative and not having a father impacted him. Sally describes his personality as that of a "pleaser," wanting to ensure that everyone is happy.

This may sound like a positive trait, but it is also reminiscent of a survivor's mindset. Sally describes the Jewish holidays that were celebrated at her parents' house. "My mother would make enough food for 80 people," she recalls with a smile in her voice before adding, "although only 40 were expected."

For Children of Survivors, the Decision to Practice Judaism is Highly Personal

Like many Jewish families, Ruth, Sally, and Lenny noticed that their parents came to the U.S. and brought with them more than just history. With the freedom to finally practice Judaism in their homes and worship at synagogue, they also shared the coveted traditions of their favorite recipes.

"The holidays and our traditional recipes always made everyone happy," reflects Sally. Lenny concurs: "Passover and Hanukkah were the times when everyone felt positive and content."

These holidays marked a period when anxiety was absent and instead, their home was filled with the scent of food, helpful hands preparing cherished dishes, and extended family of aunts, uncles, and cousins, joined together with friends, to celebrate.

Jewish cooking is a tradition that wasn't erased by the

war. "My mother would make a sponge cake for anyone who smiled at her," says Sally.

"Stuffed cabbage was another favorite among family and friends," adds Lenny.

They recall how their mother would make enough stuffed cabbage to have for dinner with ample leftovers that she would divide into smaller portions and place in baggies for freezing. Anyone who came to visit would receive a parting gift of a bag containing her delicious stuffed cabbage. This recipe was a crowd pleaser because of its many variations. One was filled with rice and beef; another contained chicken and rice; and finally, a vegetarian version with lentils and mushrooms ensured that everyone who wanted some was included.

Carrying on traditions through food and sharing helps Sally and Lenny be positive role-models for their own children. As children of Holocaust survivors, they are painfully aware that their religion and culture caused much suffering to their ancestors. For this reason, some of their friends have turned their back on religion.

"I find that our friends who carry on our Jewish traditions have a more cohesive family unit," notes Sally. "They want to prove that they are strong and continue their traditions."

However, other friends have not embraced their religion, citing that it is the cause of persecution. What everyone agrees on, however, is the pleasure they get from the sharing of food.

Lenny introduced both of his daughters to the Jewish religion and had them attend synagogue with him. While other children would go outdoors to play after the service, Lenny's eldest preferred to stay with him to take part in the temple's leadership meetings.

"I always considered myself to be conservative," says Lenny, describing the "middle" ranking of how a Jewish person sees themselves in relation to their religion. His daughter, however, maintains an Orthodox view of Judaism. "There was always a calling within her," says Lenny. I brought her to temple and the seeds were planted, but something about the Orthodox lifestyle grabbed her early, and she felt it was important."

Like her grandmother, Lenny's daughter takes care of her family and extended family members by making meals and sharing. But the quantity of food prepared is much different, and perhaps indicative of a healthier attitude.

"After the war, any time there was reason for an event, the entire community would be invited to my parents' home," says Lenny. "We always planned enough food for the whole community."

Sally notes, "Weddings were the biggest gatherings. Our parents didn't even know everyone who came, but they wanted to extend the invitation." As she explains, their parents felt so thankful for their survival that sharing happiness and food with as many as possible made them feel better."

This early tradition in their parents' marriage continued and played into why there was so much food at family holiday dinners. "We never worried if a last minute arrival turned up," explains Lenny. "There was always enough."

In contrast, Lenny's daughter estimates the number of people at her table and prepares an amount more reasonable for the number of expected guests. "She has a lot of respect for my mother," says Lenny, "but she in terms of quantity, she does not want to waste food."

Although sharing meals with many brought their mother happiness, food was also a source of Holocaust memories. The reminder that there was a time when food wasn't plentiful played into why their mother cooked with abundance. "My mother placed pans of food under her comforter to keep warm before parties," recalls Lenny. "However, because it was placed in the spare bedroom, it would sometimes be forgotten and not found for days later."

Today, these memories bring a smile to Sally and Lenny's face as they choose to focus on the happier reflections of family gatherings.

ALICE ALSO RECALLS A HAPPY UPBRINGING. AFTER the war, Alice's parents returned to their birthplace of Poland. Soon after, Alice and her brother were born, but the rampant antisemitism that existed after the war led her parents to seek a better life in Belgium. Even there, much hatred toward Jews existed so they moved again, this time to the United States. Like many others Jews, they arrived in New York and then chose to reside permanently in the Fairfax district of Los Angeles.

Growing up in Los Angeles, Alice enjoyed a stable home life with lots of love. Her parents were determined to never cause pain to their children and in that effort, they refused to speak of anything unpleasant. Alice believes their determination to avoid strife led them to be too lenient.

In high school, Alice would stay out all night without her parents ever balking. They reasoned that it wasn't Nazi occupied Poland, so she was safe. Similarly, her brother lived on the edge, experimenting with drugs and alcohol in spite of becoming a doctor. Neither were given advice on how to survive the teenager years because their parents never lived a normal teenage life. Sadly, her brother allowed his hard lifestyle to take over and lead to his early passing. As time moved forward, Alice's awareness of antisemitism increased. She became scared to let people know she was Jewish.

Now that her father has passed away, her mother has developed PTSD from the Holocaust and short-term memory failure. Without her short-term memory, her mother speaks freely about her long-term memories, reliving the horrors of the Holocaust and believing that everyone she knew was killed by the Nazis. Alice can only respond with, "Mom, I'm here."

While life is more challenging for her today, Alice recalls her childhood and younger adulthood years with a smile. Her parents always tried to give her everything. Once while in college, she called her dad needing a loan. He immediately called her professor to arrange for a small loan on the spot. She remembers fondly that her father made sure her needs were met. When asked to describe her childhood, she refers to it as blessed and happy.

Life as a child of a Holocaust survivor wasn't as good for Tama. She was raised on stories of the Holocaust. Rather than equate Judaism with culture or food, synagogue or tradition, she viewed it as part of war.

Her father was born in the town of Auschwitz, and during the course of the war, found himself in that infamous concentration camp among five other camps. He survived the concentration camps, but his time in captivity influenced his future behavior.

He believed in corporal punishment and maintained a strong, almost militant work ethic. Tama and her siblings felt as if they lived in their own concentration camp. Her sister was regularly beaten. Her brother was also beaten, presumably because he identified as being gay. Tama recalls that she never felt safe at home amongst the violence. One day, her sister climbed atop the balcony, wanting to jump in order to avoid the beatings.

Her father wanted to remember and talk about Auschwitz. When someone asked him where he went to college, he replied, "The college of Auschwitz ... better to graduate through the gates than the chimney."

By the time Tama was a teenager she rebelled against everything her father stood for. Although her father refused to take any pain medicine to relieve the permanent limp he acquired from concentration camp beatings, Tama began to self-medicate with alcohol and opiates. Her rebellious nature caused so many problems that she was sent to a boarding school at age 17. Another act of rebellion was her decision to marry a man who wasn't Jewish.

Whenever Tama or her siblings played too loudly, a beating would ensue. During family dinners, her father's belt sat at the ready on the edge of his chair. Tama and her brother taught their dog to take the belt away, but that only worked some of the time. When her father would beat them, if they didn't cry he questioned whether they understood the punishment and would hit again. Their mother wasn't any better, and together, their parents presented a dangerous front.

To the outside world, however, they appeared as the

perfect family. The children were neat and clean. The parents were beloved. And, Tama wanted to maintain this smokescreen. But one day, Tama's friend visited and Tama neglected to wash the dishes in the manner that her father preferred. He flew into a rage. Her friend left and never returned.

When her own children were born, Tama asked her father how he could have beaten his kids. He insisted that he never did this. Although it wasn't an acknowledgement or apology, her father finally became the person he should have always been. When her children asked him about the numbers tattooed on his arm, he lied and said it was an ex-girlfriend's phone number. He had developed a more gentle demeanor and wanted to spare the grandchildren of sadness.

Tama wishes his epiphany had come sooner so that his own children could have grown up in a happy home. After her father's death, her emotions spiraled and addiction to drugs and alcohol plagued her. She recalls that she even stole her dad's Vicodin pills after his funeral. Since then, Tama has worked hard to quit drugs and alcohol, yet acknowledges that the usage helped her escape the pain.

※

Like Tama, her sister, Shelly, had a difficult upbringing. They grew up in alien circumstances with parents who were both detached and abusive. She experienced psychological and physical brutality.

She was raised to accept that Judaism was the only acceptable belief system. Yet, Shelly learned early on that her parents used Judaism as what she referred to as a social tool. When the family was in public, her parents presented an appearance of a perfect, happy unit. The reality at home was far different with her parents using religion as a means to control.

When Shelly tried out and was accepted onto her high school drill team, she was expected and looked forward to attending Friday night games. Immediately, her father decided the family would attend temple on Friday nights.

She didn't dare refuse her father's wishes because to do so would mean enduring violence at his hand. The abuse was so frequent that she developed PTSD like symptoms including regular nightmares. Her trauma didn't stem only from the abuse she experienced, but also from being forced to watch her father beat her siblings. Making matters worse, her mother seemed to encourage it.

The hypocrisy of the family's make-believe happy stature in public compared to abusive actions in the home permeated Shelly's view of religion. When she went to graduate school her father became angry because he wanted her to be a rabbi. Shelly refused because she knew her family was not an example of how Jews should live. She recognized that she was given no tools to navigate life and felt psychologically unprepared for her future let alone counsel others.

Shelly got married at 20 to get out of the house. The marriage lasted one year. She remarried a second time to a man who was good looking and gave her whatever she wanted at first. She thought she had won the lottery, but soon discovered she was merely a well dressed slave. Her life with this man was similar to her upbringing. Everything looked great on the outside, but inside there was abuse. He would tell her he took her from the gutter.

Years later, on a rare occasion when her father tried to have a conversation with her, she asked why he hit her. Similar to what he told her sister, Tama, he insisted that abuse never occurred. She exclaimed, "How can you blame the Germans for torturing you when you can't admit to hitting your own kids?" After that conversation, her father refused to speak to her for six months.

Shelly feels her Jewishness provided nothing positive in her life, but in actuality, a torturous upbringing resulting in 20 years of therapy seeking. Her first therapist was Jewish and said she needed to understand what her father went through. She never returned to his office. The next therapist said Shelly's issues were greater than she was trained to handle.

After her father's death in 2002, Shelly found the freedom to pursue her own beliefs, receive her PhD, and follow the teachings of a guru. She believes this allowed her to escape from being a xenophobic, insular Jew.

As a disciple of the guru, she practiced meditation and discovered a world outside of her bubble. She even became more compassionate of her father. She wakes up and feels grateful for her life. Her guru used to say memories should be put in storage and only pulled out when they are needed. She now lives life on her terms. She doesn't depend on her family or a man for her validation.

At the time of this writing, Shelly's mother is 83. One day her mother said she had read in the *Jewish Journal* that children of holocaust survivors had psychological issues. She asked Shelly if she had any issues. She didn't want to pursue the conversation so Shelly answered no. Her mother responded, "Good because your father would be very upset." Shelly has so much resentment towards her because of the abuse. She doesn't want to hurt her mother now so she doesn't see her.

Shelly was trained to tell her parents she loved them when she never meant it. Now she's learned to only say I love you when the words hold value. Shelly realizes that not every Holocaust survivor is the epitome of Eli Weisel. Not all survivors are heroes. They are just people who had terrible experiences thrust upon them.

Chapter 3

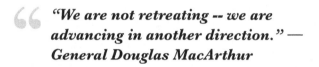 **"We are not retreating -- we are advancing in another direction." — General Douglas MacArthur**

While Jews in Europe were being persecuted during World War II, other Jews who had previously come to the United States were living in a very different situation. Between the years of 1820 through 1920, a steady flow of Jewish immigrants came to the U.S. Most came from Central Europe to settle on the East Coast in New York, Philadelphia, and Baltimore. Some made their way to Cincinnati, Cleveland, Louisville, Minneapolis, St. Louis, New Orleans, San Francisco, and small towns scattered throughout the U.S. However, this influx of immigration ended with new, restrictive laws passed in 1921 and 1924.

Under President Franklin D. Roosevelt, more Jews than ever before entered public life. Yet, even those who lived in the U.S. often faced antisemitism and discrimination during the period of World War II and continuing after. Additionally, during the war, debate occurred on whether Jewish leaders in the United States were doing enough to help the persecuted in Europe. Some felt more pressure should have been placed on the government to help; others believed nothing more could be done.

Although this debate was intense, nobody could argue with the fact that in 1945, the U.S. housed the most politically important and largest Jewish community in the world. Still, new generations of Jews were shaped by their ancestors' hardships.

What was it like to not only be an immigrant, but also to carry the label of "survivor"? Were these survivors able to enjoy the new life they had forged?

MODERN VIEWS OF GERMANY

Betty's mother became a prisoner of a concentration camp at age 14. She was liberated at 16. Similarly, her father spent time in the camps, but survived without any permanent physical damage. Although her parents didn't realize it, mental damage remained.

Her father poured himself into work rather than spend much time with family. His focus distracted him from his memories. Looking back, Betty realizes her father was oddly unemotional and likely depressed. Her mother took on the role of protecting the children from him as he had little patience. When Betty asked a question that bothered him, his response was to spank her. Betty learned her parents were survivors; and subsequently, learned not to ask questions.

Although she distanced herself from her father, Betty was close to her mother. When she started dating, Betty asked her mother how to kiss, and her mother explained in detail without any embarrassment. She wanted Betty to experience everything in life that she had missed out on. As such, she never asked Betty to help around the house with cooking or cleaning. When she married at age 19, she had no idea how to perform common household tasks.

Unlike many survivors, her parents didn't hold a lot of resentment towards the Germans. When Betty wanted to buy her first car, she eyed a Volkswagen, but assumed her father wouldn't approve. Yet, he responded that the war was 25 years ago and the Germans had made reparations.

Betty thought that they had overcome their difficulties and that she also came out unscathed. However, when she dated a man who was an Orthodox Jew and a psychiatrist, he told Betty that he recognized many classic traits found in children of Holocaust survivors including being overly protective and nurturing along with type A traits.

꙼

ALTHOUGH BETTY'S FATHER MOVED FORWARD AND even agreed to buy German products, Sandy's father made the decision to boycott German products.

He originated from Transylvania and the Holocaust left a permanent toll on his personality. Sandy recalls that he would talk to anyone who would listen about the Holocaust, even her friends from elementary school. When she reached middle school age, he spoke to the class about this gruesome part of history, but was careful to never admit he was Sandy's father due to a leftover fear that the Nazis could still be lurking and find her.

His guilt of surviving plagued him throughout his life.

His job in the concentration camp was to escort other prisoners into the gas chamber. The memory made him always look over his shoulder, afraid that any surviving Jews would find out and come after him.

The family decision to boycott all German products impacted Sandy. One Chanukah, she received the Barbie dream house she wanted, but when her father discovered it was made in Germany, he took it away.

It didn't matter that Sandy was devastated. Her father insisted that she be informed about the Holocaust and his beliefs. He had her watch documentaries on the subject and went so far as to tell her she would never survive what he went through.

⚘

The Impact on Future Relationships

Sarah also experienced long-term psychological trauma and passed on damaging issues. She lost a seven-year-old daughter when they became separated due to the Holocaust. Once the war was over and she had journeyed to the United States, she maintained her hope of being reunited.

This hope was most likely in vain, but it never waned. For years, she would imagine seeing her daughter. Once when she was on a train, she saw a young girl who appeared to be the same age as her daughter should have been at the time. Sarah approached the girl. This behavior continued whenever she saw someone with similar features to her daughter.

Although she had continued with life and had another child, the memories of the Holocaust were too strong and affected the way she raised her second daughter. She never allowed her to go out alone. She feared her daughter might become lost or be taken. Even simple household chores were strictly monitored. Sarah never allowed her daughter to do the laundry for fear that she might become mangled or harmed from the machinery.

Protecting her daughter at any cost became Sarah's driving force. She wore bandages over her number tattoo to hide it from her daughter. She also kept an ample amount of cash — $1,000 — pinned within her bra. This money was hidden from plain view, both from sight of strangers and her daughter — but never forgotten. It was there with Sarah, close to her body, in case war would break out suddenly or an incident occurred where she would need it at a moment's notice.

The war had created many scars beyond this behavior and her tattoo. While in the concentration camps, Sarah was raped. This act instilled lifelong fear in her that also translated to her parenting behaviors. When Sarah's daughter was 18 and an adult, she asked for permission to date. Sarah denied her request, stating that she wasn't physically strong enough.

When her daughter insisted that nothing would happen and if it did, she was strong enough, Sarah's response was to throw her down on a bed, spread her legs, and then having gained the unwanted proof that she feared, Sarah stated, "You see? You aren't strong enough."

＊

BEATRICE'S DAD, FRANKIE, WAS A CHILD WHEN HE was sent to the concentration camps with his parents. He and his mother, Malka, survived, but Frankie's life remained far from easy.

Malka developed anger issues and would beat Frankie with pots and pans. In response, Frankie became a shell of a person, remaining silent during the attacks and adopting a demeanor without any emotion in other areas of his life.

As he got older, he entered into a marriage arranged by Malka to a woman named Phyllis, who had not been a Holocaust prisoner. The dramatic change in the way Frankie and Phyllis were raised affected their marriage, and in spite of having a child, Beatrice, their relationship was strained. When Beatrice was 17, she learned that her father had kept a long term girlfriend.

Phyllis accepted the indiscretion because Frankie needed more physical attention than she was willing to give. However, Beatrice asked her father to leave their house. Phyllis would not divorce him. Instead, Beatrice and her father attended counseling. The therapist told them both that his affair was not unusual because of the trauma he endured from the Holocaust as a child. During therapy, he also revealed that his step-brothers had forced him to have sex with their maids. With this additional information, Beatrice stopped attending therapy.

She developed weight issues and had relationship problems of her own. Like her father, she kept her emotions close. Recognizing that she had adopted some behaviors from her parents, Beatrice swore she would never end up like them.

One day, Frankie was cleaning out his brother's apartment in Manhattan after he had passed away. Phyllis was shopping with her mother-in-law, Malka, in the city and stopped by unexpectedly. She discovered Frankie having sex. Although she knew of his affair and girlfriend, witnessing them together destroyed her self-esteem and she turned on her family.

Throughout their family ordeals, Beatrice's maternal grandmother was a rare source of encouragement. Her parents had a check cashing business and used their money as a means of controlling Beatrice. She turned away from the family business as a result. Her grandmother convinced Beatrice to go to college and cared for her when her own parents seemed unable to show any love.

Yet, in spite of receiving love from her grandmother, Beatrice never felt she would find love or get married. She was pleasantly surprised to meet Oscar in her 30s and, like her grandmother, he provided the love she never knew from her parents.

When Beatrice's grandmother passed away, she came home from college. Her father did not return home, leaving Phyllis alone to grieve. By this time, Phyllis had accepted his relationship with his girlfriend, and she and Beatrice recognized that even in death, he could show no emotion.

After the war, Frankie's mother, Malka, was married seven times. He never knew his dad.

❦

Whereas Sarah showed extreme over-protectiveness of her daughter. In contrast, Frankie's mother beat him. His reaction was to show no reaction. Lack of emotion is another common response among survivors as they navigate their life after the war. Sally and Lenny's parents, particularly their father, was such a person.

Sally was well aware that her parents were robbed of their childhood because of enduring the Holocaust. As a result, she never wanted to tell her parents if she felt sad or even if she experienced happiness. "They never spoke to me about their childhood, but I knew it wasn't good and they didn't have anything nice growing up. I kept my emotions to myself because I didn't want to hurt them," she says.

Lenny agrees stating, "Our emotions were very tempered." Yet, one day he admitted to his father that he was being bullied at school. His father confronted the kids, who were older than Lenny. He recognizes that this sort of behavior in a parent wouldn't fly today, but his father's background wouldn't allow for anyone to resort to bullying.

"Fathers are role-models, especially for sons," says Lenny. "I'm similar to my dad in that I don't show a lot of emotion, but I do make sure my kids know they are loved."

Sally admits, "I never told my parents that I loved them, yet I never hang up the phone with my kids without saying I love you."

Both Sally and Lenny believe that their parents' lack of stoicism stems from wanting to protect them. They recognize the difficulty their parents felt when emotions would take over. In their words: "If they allowed themselves to get emotional, the feelings might get away from them."

To celebrate their parents' 25th wedding anniversary, Sally and Lenny held a party at their house. When gifts were being opened, their parents exchanged a kiss. It was a huge deal for the family to see the rare display of affection.

"We always knew that our parents felt tremendous pride for us," says Sally. Lenny concurs, "If something either good or bad happened to us, it was as if the whole world stood still."

When Lenny married and their eldest sister, Ruth, couldn't attend due to her severe agoraphobia, their father cried knowing the illness was another aftermath of the Holocaust. Family events, most notably a wedding, were meant to be shared. The family placed tremendous value on this ideal particularly when they had lost so many family members in the war. Sally remembers that it was the only time she had ever seen their father cry.

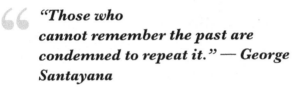

Chapter 4

"Those who cannot remember the past are condemned to repeat it." — George Santayana

For many Jewish people, their religion is as much about culture, community, and family as it is about religion. Today's families of multi-generational Jews take pride in their cultural and personal histories — the good times and the bad. It is, in fact, a driving reason for the writing of this book.

History is often defined as the study of change over time. Change is not always obvious. It occurs in vast aspects of our lives. Analyzing the Holocaust brings up studies of religious change as well as political, social, and military change. But these changes are not exclusive of other historical changes such as economic, scientific, technological, and medical.

An intellectual paper published by Valdosta State University in Georgia discussed the difference in the study of history between historians versus non-historians. In it, the author wrote:

> *"Non-historians often say that 'history repeats itself' or that 'things were always this way.' History cannot repeat itself because history is not a living, thinking being. History is an intellectual discipline practiced by historians who try to make sense of the past. Because history is about change, nothing was ever "always" a certain way.*

The author presents a valid argument and yet, it is one that can be debated. We see other genocides throughout the world implying that history most certainly repeats. Many areas in the world are experiencing ethnic cleansing. While the numbers are not as high as the Holocaust, they cannot be ignored.

Fear of widespread harm occurs in the following locales and against the following groups:

Darfuris in Sudan

Ethnic killings began in 2003 when Arab militias began massacring non-Arab people. The genocide is supported by Sudan's President Omar Hassan al-Bashir.

Christians and Muslims in the Central African Republic

In 2013, the Central African Republic (Democratic Republic of the Congo, South Sudan, and Chad) became involved in a civil war that escalated when the country's Christian President François Bozizé was overthrown by a coalition of Muslim groups. The war subsided in 2016, but ethnic tensions grew and the United Nations believes genocide is occurring between the anti-Balaka Christian militias and the Muslim coalition.

CHRISTIANS AND YAZIDIS IN IRAQ AND SYRIA

The terrorist group ISIS systematically attempted to exterminate Yazidis, Shiites, and Christians in Syria and Iraq from 2014-2015.

THE NUER AND OTHER ETHNIC GROUPS IN SOUTH SUDAN

As a result of a 2005 agreement that ended Africa's longest civil war, South Sudan gained independence from Sudan and became a country in itself in 2011. However, the independence did not free South Sudan from conflict.

South Sudan's President Salva Kiir began using his army to ethnically kill the Nuer and other smaller local groups, who are rivals to his own political group, the Dinka. The Nuer have taken part in ethnic cleansing against the Dinka as well.

THE ROHINGYA IN MYANMAR

In northwestern Myanmar, Muslims known as the Rohingya have long suffered as second class citizens. In 2017, U.S. Secretary of State Rex Tillerson declared that ethnic cleansing was being committed against the Rohingya Muslims. In 2018, a United Nations report accused Myanmar's military leaders of carrying out genocide, war crimes, and crimes against humanity on this group. Six generals were to face trial at the International Criminal Court and Aung San Suu Kyi was accused of failing to prevent violence. However, Myanmar rejected the findings and retaliated by sentencing two Reuters journalists to prison for violating state secrecy laws.

At the time of this writing in 2021, genocide watches take place in:

- Burundi
- Central African Republic
- India (Kashmir, Assam State)
- Iraq (ISIS, Hashd al-shaabi, Turkey)
- Myanmar (Rakhine, Kachin)
- Nigeria (Boko Haram, Borno State)
- Somalia
- Sudan South Sudan
- Turkey/Syria/Iraq (Turkish army, Anatolia, Afrin, Sinjar, Nineveh)
- Yemen (Saudi Arabia, Houthi rebels)

In areas where it is possible, family members speak out to the media. The reports prove that these horrific incidents have long-reaching effects not only on the people who have been brutalized, but also their family members. In Shariya Camp, Iraq, an uncle nurses his 16-year-old niece back to health after she was rescued. She escaped the Islamic State after three years of captivity, taken by ISIS and serial raped in Mosul. Although she escaped and is back home, he tells her story because none of them can escape the memories.

Even within the United States, discrimination occurs. What is perhaps most upsetting is that like the countries listed above, much of this discrimination stems from our leadership.

The Women's March, held on January 21, 2017 — the day after the inauguration of President Donald Trump — was the largest single-day protest in U.S. history. It resulted due to statements he made that were considered anti-women and offensive.

Organizers set a goal to bring attention and advocate for human rights and other issues including women's rights, immigration reform, healthcare reform, reproductive rights, the environment, LGBTQ rights, racial equality, workers' rights, and most notable for this particular writing — freedom of religion and tolerance.

※

"THE MORE THINGS CHANGE...THE MORE THEY STAY THE SAME."

Mike's father was an American soldier who was captured during the Battle of the Bulge. His service issued dog tag revealed he was Jewish, and subsequently, he was sent to Stalag IX-B, northwest of Frankfurt. As a prisoner, he was transported in a train under similar conditions as European Jews. His destination was Berga, a sub-camp of Buchenwald.

Berga was a quaint German town of 7,000 people, but the prisoners in Berga were slave laborers. The Germans took the prisoners on a 140-mile death march. Hungarian Jews were often executed during these marches, and in fact, Mike's dad had a gun held to the back of his head, but he was saved by an SS agent.

Mike's father told him about his experiences when he was old enough to understand. Ever since, Mike heard the stories of what occurred in Europe and was warned it could happen in America. As a result, Mike kept his passport up to date fearing that if needed, he would escape to Israel.

In addition to sharing his story with his son, Mike's dad made it a point to tell others, believing he had a responsibility to do so in order for the Holocaust not be forgotten. Yet, in his quest to share his story, he often got into arguments with people who believed the stories were overblown. He would respond that they had no idea what it was like to have a gun held to the back of their head or witness hundreds of Jews gunned down in front of them.

Mike's dad developed a cold demeanor. When Mike's loving cat died, Mike was devastated. His father told him to get over it. One night, Mike heard his mother screaming. He ran into his parents' room to find his father choking her, dreaming that he was strangling a German soldier.

On another occasion, Mike went through a glass door and was badly cut. His mother cried and showed her concern; his father picked him up and like a soldier told to leave nobody behind, he rushed him to a doctor, but showed no emotion.

Mike has spent most of his life studying history and the Holocaust. He still believes that a similar occurrence can and will happen in the United States, holding onto the adage, "The more things change, the more they stay the same."

JEWISH RIGHTS AND TOLERANCE

Will there be a movement for tolerance of Jews? Should there be? Is it needed? In 2018, Julie Zauzmer, a reporter covering politics and religion for the *Washington Post*, interviewed Jewish teens in America following a mass shooting at Tree of Life synagogue in Pittsburgh.

Millennials spoke to her about the first time in their lives that they felt fear over being Jewish. Yael Fisher said she had never felt scared to be Jewish before, but now recognized that she could be in physical danger.

Hayley Berger agreed with Fisher, recalling the time

she realized there were Americans who hate Jews so much that they could commit murder. She recalled a time earlier in 2014 when a white supremacist fatally shot three people outside the Jewish Community Center and a Jewish retirement home where she lived in Kansas.

Reuben Siegman told Zauzmer that he realized people targeted Jews when a Jewish cemetery in his home town of St. Louis was vandalized. The same thing happened at a Jewish cemetery in Philadelphia.

Their stories have more in common than simply reporting antisemitism. These Millennials acknowledged that they grew up learning about anti-Semitism, mainly in the context of school lessons about the Holocaust, Eastern European pogroms, and the Spanish Inquisition, along with stories from their parents and grandparents. However, in their words, they "didn't think that these things happened today." As they told the *Washington Post*, they believed these were stories from "history books about events that happened well over half a century ago, and all in the old country, not the United States."

In this modern day, it's hard for many to believe that antisemitism still exists. Yet, we have the Black Lives Matter movement as evidence that hatred still runs rampant. This hate transcends races, cultures, and certainly religions in other countries and in the United States.

Following the synagogue shooting in Pittsburgh, an Irvine, California temple was desecrated with the words "F--- Jews" painted on the walls. A similar hate crime occurred inside a Brooklyn synagogue with "Kill All Jews" written.

Racism and antisemitism also is rampant on the internet. A seemingly innocuous google search may have resulted in antisemitic images that are disturbing beyond the concept of racism. Searching the term "Jewish Baby Stroller" allegedly resulted in images of portable ovens.

Google investigated the findings and according to an article appearing in September of 2020 from The Times of Israel: "The Network Contagion Research Institute, which studies the way hate speech spreads online, located a series of posts on the '4chan' message board, dating back to 2017."

The social media platform, Twitter, overflows with daily antisemitic messages that attract billions of views. Years after the Holocaust, we may wonder what kind of people spread these messages. The answer can lie with those who accept the messages or turn the other cheek. When neo-Nazis marched in Charlottesville chanting "Jews will not replace us," most public officials immediately called the display an act of racism, bigotry, hatred, vileness, intolerance, violence, and more. Trump limply called it "sad".

If history doesn't repeat itself, then it certainly mirrors itself. As this book has demonstrated, the effects of the Holocaust are not limited to the people who lived through it, but also extending to their children.

Those children who believe that their relatives' deaths should not be in vane, work tirelessly to share their history and culture with others. Fortunately, as time places more distance between our memories and the Holocaust, sharing history also extends to happier conversations, joyful gatherings, and shared cultural experiences, which we will explore more in the next chapter.

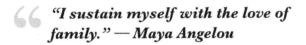

Chapter 5

"I sustain myself with the love of family." — Maya Angelou

One of the most loved cultural exchanges among Jewish people is through food. The recipes of our deceased relatives and friends live on and are, in fact, passed along to new generations. The Jewish food culture is celebrated in homes and at various delis throughout the United States with some of the most famous of these delis being in Los Angeles and New York.

In the early part of the last century, many Jewish businesses were established and still survive today. Canter's Deli originally opened in Boyle Heights in 1931. In 1953, the famed deli moved to the site of the old Esquire theater building on Fairfax Boulevard in Los Angeles. It soon became a landmark in itself and one of the city's first 24-hour restaurants.

To this day, the culinary landmark is managed by third and fourth-generations of the Canter family. Its history began even before it opened in Boyle Heights. Originally, the family launched a small storefront deli in Jersey City, New Jersey in 1924. With the stock market crash of 1929, the business was lost. Soon after, Ben Canter and his two brothers moved to California. They had only $500, but it was enough to launch their Boyle Heights location and make a success out of it. With the offerings of Canter's Deli, this location became the Jewish center of Los Angeles.

Nate and Al's Deli of Beverly Hills soon followed suit and opened in 1945. It was the collaboration between friends and business partners Nate Rimer and Al Mendelson. The business was run by their families for three generation. In February 2018, there was fear that the restaurant would close as the original owners planned to sell. In January 2019, an investor group made up of Rande Gerber and Cindy Crawford, Mike Meldman, Jeff Shell, and Jay Sures purchased the deli and kept its doors open.

Brent's Delicatessen & Restaurant launched in a small storefront in Northridge, California in the heart of the San Fernando Valley. It was originally opened in 1967, but then purchased by Ron Peskin in 1969 for just $1,700. Ron and his wife, Patricia, started with one delivery truck and 11 employees. Today, the deli boasts a second location in Westlake Village, also in California, and is considered one of the best delis in the state and perhaps nation.

Factor's isn't just any deli, but as its name states, it is Factor's Famous Deli. It has stood at its Pico Boulevard location in Los Angeles since 1948. Owned and operated by the Markowitz family since 1969, Herman and Lili

Markowitz started the deli and now their children carry on their parents' commitment to quality food and friendly service.

Although the Factor's Famous Deli website gives customers a sliver of its history, it does not reveal that Herman and Lili survived the Holocaust. Their four children are cousins to Sally and Lenny and shared some of their family's untold history.

※

AN EYE FOR BUSINESS — FRIENDS HELPING FRIENDS

In its early days, the deli was not the thriving business that it is today. Sally and Lenny's father may not have had a formal business education, but he had a mind for business. He understood what was needed to make a business successful and in the case of a deli, it started with the food.

At Herman and Lili's request, he analyzed their business and determined that the meat they bought wasn't high enough quality to attract a loyal following. He offered to supply them with better meat and provide a financial loan.

His business, Sam's Meat Market, was located on Fairfax Boulevard between Pico and Olympic. He had already made a success of this business and knew how to help Herman and Lili. His good business sense also led him to make wise investments. Whenever he had the resources, he would buy property.

He bought the butcher shop property along with the two stores on either side of it. When the landlord for the properties wanted to raise the rent, Lenny's father complained. The landlord suggested he make him an offer to buy the land and he did exactly that. It was a low offer, but accepted nonetheless.

These three properties were bought between 1970 and 1977, and by 1988 at the time of his death, all three were paid off. He also purchased a duplex, preferring a property where he could collect rent to owning a single family home. "My father serviced any repairs needed on the duplex himself," said Lenny. "He took pride in it and although he could have hired someone to help, nobody would meet his strong expectations."

Their mother also did her part. When she would visit their tenants, inevitably coffee would be served and they would spend quality time together. "It was a business of love," says Lenny.

Sally and Lenny's father worked 15 hour days, six days a week in his butcher shop. But his hard work bene-fitted his family and others like the Factors Deli owners. "I remember him being so tired upon getting home that he would sit in his chair and go to sleep," recalls Lenny.

Lenny also recalls him being kind, but with a temper. "He was authoritative," Lenny says simply. Like many children, Lenny and his siblings didn't appreciate all of his father's decisions. "Today, our memories of him are good, but when growing up, we didn't understand every-thing," admits Lenny. "Dad had a great sense of humor, but he was careful of what he said and to whom he said it. Now, everything makes a bit more sense. In looking at what he endured during the Holocaust, his behavior is understandable."

Yet, as a survivor of the concentration camps, Lenny and Sally describe their dad as hardened. They learned that he survived the camps by his wit and strength. Like his sister, Ruth, Lenny worked in the butcher shop during his college breaks at the holiday season and in summer. During alone times, their dad would talk about the concentration camp.

He described in painful detail what he endured including being put in a box only big enough for him to stand. Trying to sit was impossible because there simply wasn't room. Spikes surrounded the walls making it impossible to move. He would be forced to stay in that box for hours.

When asked how much of what he endured during the Holocaust played into his father's personality, Lenny debates the concept of nature versus nurture. He believes his father could not have embodied his strong will, tenacity, or desire to succeed if it had not always been a part of his personality. These traits, Lenny and Sally believe, are within a person from the beginning, but can be magnified by one's experiences.

"Our father would rarely reference the Holocaust," says Sally. "We knew it was important for people to remember it, but he didn't talk about it."

Prior to the Holocaust, their father was raised in a very religious Jewish household. Born in 1924 in Riatna, (near Chust) Chekoslovakia, he lived in Israel from 1949 to 1954. He was president of his synagogue and grew up in a very modest home. They would even go to the forest to cut a tree for their own firewood. The family traditions started by their father are carried on by Lenny today.

"I remember when an aunt and uncle of mine passed away. My first thought was to plant a tree in their honor," says Lenny.

This was perhaps an instinct that was cultivated by

their grandfather, another inherited legacy. And as for the traits that their father embodied, Lenny and Sally's friends remember him in the same way that the Factor's Famous Deli family does — as a man who would help anyone.

※

BUILDING A BETTER LIFE

Anna Muravina Langsam was born in Ukraine in 1923 while it was still part of the USSR. Harry "Yecheskel" Langsam was born in Poland in 1921. They were deemed "lucky" to have survived in Siberia during the war.

Anna was evacuated from Kiev and Harry and his brother escaped from Poland. Both managed to make their way east to Siberia where they met, fell in love, and got married in 1945. After the war, they returned west to learn who had survived. Many of their relatives had perished. Harry lost his father as well as his married sister and her family. Anna lost her brother, who was in the Red Army, along with a married sister and her family. Harry and Anna stayed in a Displaced Persons Camp in Germany where their first daughter, Rema, was born in 1947. Two years later, they emigrated to the new State of Israel and Anna gave birth to another baby girl, Esther.

Life in Israel in the 1950s was difficult with food shortages, hard work, a war, and the Sinai Campaign of 1956. In 1957, when Esther was eight and Rema was ten, their parents chose to emigrate to the United States and chose to live in Los Angeles where Harry had another sister close by.

Living in America created new demands. Esther recalls that her Eastern European parents were consumed with working hard in order to build a better life. Initially, Esther's father worked as a construction laborer helping to build the freeway system. He saved money and later became the owner of a small luncheonette downtown, but its eventual closure forced him to change directions. Because the war had interrupted his studies, he relied on his wiles and self-education. He found work as a clerk with the Bank of California.

While in Siberia, Esther's mother worked as a civil servant, but because English was her second language, once in Los Angeles she settled for working as a seamstress in not much more than a sweatshop. Yet, as is the mentality of most Holocaust survivors, she never complained about the hard work.

Money was tight for the family, but Harry and Anna were determined to always put food on the table and save for a house, choosing the Fairfax district like many other Jewish friends. Esther typically wore Rema's hand-me-down clothing, which were often loaned from someone previous even to Rema. Birthday presents were scarce and restaurant dining was even rarer. Yet, Esther recalls her childhood as being happy.

Although they did not have many family members nearby as most stayed in Israel, they adopted an extended family of friends with similar backgrounds — most also survivors. These friends took pleasure in gathering to celebrate any occasion whether it was a birthday, anniversary, or simply that they were alive.

Believing that hardship and survival were best left in the past, her parents rarely spoke of the war. However, their European culture made assimilation in the United States more difficult. Esther befriended American born schoolmates, but always felt different. She didn't take part in Girl Scouts or summer camp.

While they studied the basics at school, at home they learned as much as they could about the American middle class by watching *Ed Sullivan, Father Knows Best, and Leave It to Beaver*. "This was our source of learning how to live in America," recalls Esther.

Eventually, her parents' dream of home ownership came to fruition. They bought a duplex and rented out the second unit to help pay the mortgage. The "American dream" was becoming a reality as they were able to not only have a home, but also a car, take day trips to parks and the beach and make special visits to Disneyland, Knott's Berry Farm, and the Pacific Ocean Park. And, like many other Jews, food was an integral part of their social life and their weekends were filled with an ethic to enjoy life fully.

Even Esther's friends enjoyed being at her home, finding her parents to be warm and welcoming. As Esther grew up, got married and had her own children, the tragedy of the war receded. Occasionally, her father would share stories of the past, but his sense of humor came through whether because he enjoyed telling a joke or to protect those he loved.

Esther is one of the fortunate children of survivors who grew up with love and benefitted from her parents' emphasis on family. Although she ensures that her refrigerator and pantry are always well stocked and she watches her spending, those lessons do not bring up feelings of pain. She enjoyed a better education than either of her parents, but paid for it herself as she didn't want to burden them with the cost. She and her late husband, Mike, enjoyed life and traveled extensively. Together, they created a beautiful life for their own children, who received loving attention from her parents, making up for the fact that Esther didn't have grandparents of her own.

Chapter 6

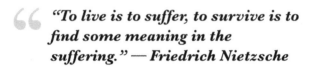 *"To live is to suffer, to survive is to find some meaning in the suffering."* — *Friedrich Nietzsche*

When considering what restaurant to frequent for a nosh or a full blown meal, the decision to go to a Jewish deli for a sandwich and a slice of chocolate babka is an easy choice that probably every Jew is happy to make. However, raising a family in the Jewish tradition, complete with keeping Kosher, training for a Bar or Bat Mitzvah, and sharing the mindset to "marry Jewish" are harder lessons that many Jews today decide aren't vital.

Alex, a friend of Sally's from her high school days, now works as a dentist in a prospering city north of Los Angeles and has a family of his own. Outward appearances do not show the difficulty that he has experienced or the far-reaching effects that the Holocaust has had on second generations.

His half-sister, Felicia, was born in 1943. Her family lived in the Warsaw ghetto. This was an area of just slightly more than one square mile where over 400,000 Jews were confined to live after the German invasion of Poland in September 1939.

Felicia's mother befriended an elderly couple who had the means to smuggle Felicia out of the ghetto via a coffin that contained other bodies. She was hidden in their basement for the duration of the war.

Alex's son researched their family on the website Ancestry.com and discovered that his dad had a surviving brother living in Brazil as well as cousins. However, the happy news of finding family was tempered with the reality of Alex's difficulty growing up with his parents, who he describes as "difficult."

His father would have outbursts and make scenes. When they were in public, Alex resorted to pretending he didn't know his parents. His father's behavior, coupled with Alex's lies, affected his self esteem. When asked to provide other details about his father, Alex replied, "My dad was an asshole; my goal is to be less of an asshole."

His father's rants and warnings certainly didn't help his psychological well-being. Alex recalls his father telling him, "You think you're safe. The day you forget you're a Jew is when they will get you." His explosive personality resulted in his father being kicked out of three temples.

Felicia seemed able to shield herself from the family dynamics having gained a modeling job with Max Factor, but the ability to land this coveted job was merely a facade. Mental illness soon plagued her. Felicia became a paranoid schizophrenic and was institutionalized. Alex felt tremendous guilt over his inability to help her.

Alex continued to seek answers to the mysteries of his family. When he met his aunt for the first time after his mother died, she told him quite simply that his mother was a bitch. However, she added that being a bitch saved her life.

The Gestapo, secret police of Nazi Germany, would frequently barge into homes looking for Jews. His mother found out it was going to happen in their neighborhood. They had a hole in the dining room floor ready as a hiding place. When they heard the Gestapo, she pulled her sister under the hole and covered it with a carpet. Her sister (Alex's aunt) started to cry and Alex's mother put her hands around her sister's neck telling her that if she made a sound, she would snap her neck. The soldiers left without discovering them.

After the war, Alex's mother searched for Felicia and found her in a displaced person camp in an orphanage. Felicia's father was killed.

Alex's father told him many stories of the war. He was a partisan fighter and once saw soldiers kill an entire truck of small children. When it occurred, he was hiding and could do nothing to help. He couldn't stop his tears afterward.

When the war finally ended, Alex's father got involved with the bootleg industry. He made money smuggling illegal weapons and refugees to Haifa.

Alex describes his parents as "two crazy people with fiery tempers." They divorced when Alex was nine.

Prior to then, Alex was raised to be Orthodox, but rebelled and strayed from Judaism until recently. Today, he goes to temple three times a week.

❧

Must We Practice Judaism to be Considered Jewish?

Steven's father, a Holocaust survivor, was very violent. Steven came to believe that there are two kinds of survivors: those who speak openly about their experiences and those who refuse to talk. Yet, both can hold onto their anger and carry it forward to their own children.

Steven's father talked about the Holocaust and it affected his behavior toward his son. When Steven was eight-years-old, he went with his father to an Indian Guide campout held in Big Bear. Some of the kids wanted to ride snowmobiles, but their fathers wouldn't let them. Steven's father let him go and earned the image of being the cool dad.

But when it was time for bed, Steven wanted the top bunk. His dad repeatedly said no, but finally agreed. When Steven woke up, his friends watched him try unsuccessfully to get out of bed. He couldn't move. His father had taken rope and tied him to the bed. Steven was humiliated.

Later, he learned that while in the camps, one of his father's bunk mates was asleep in the top bunk and fell out resulting in a broken leg. No longer able to work, he was deemed a burden and the SS soldiers shot him.

Steven knew that growing up with his father as a survivor brought much trauma onto his own life. He wanted to marry someone free of those emotions. He married a woman who was beautiful inside and out, and not an offspring of a survivor.

***

IT'S PROBABLY SAFE TO SAY THAT ALL JEWS KNOW that "never forget" relates to the Holocaust, and one of the best ways to ensure that lives weren't taken in vain is to maintain the Jewish religion and culture. Yet, as with Alex, outside factors and memories can change one's decision to be actively involved with a temple. Sometimes the desire to do the right thing and never forget becomes muddied with falling in love with a non-Jew, deciding that a cheeseburger is too good to ignore, or that religion and spirituality do not have to be found in a temple.

Even though they are children of Holocaust survivors, the households that Sally and Lenny created as adults were very different. Each raised their own children with Judaism in mind, and yet in very different aspects. Does it lessen their devotion to Judaism? Does it reduce their awareness of the Holocaust? If anything, both connected the dots to determine that as children of Holocaust survivors, they each endured certain difficulties that were passed on, and both hope that one day the cycle will end.

"In the manner that I was raised, I personally would not have considered marrying someone who wasn't Jewish," says Sally.

However, it's interesting to note that she doesn't hold the same standard for her children, two sons who at the time of this writing, both have girlfriends who are not from the Jewish faith. This fact has been the subject of discussion with her friends.

Sally's best friend, a woman she has known since the age of ten and she considers akin to a sister, asked about Sally's son's choices in partners. Her friend expressed surprise citing that considering what Sally's parents endured, she would have thought marrying outside of the Jewish faith would be forbidden. Her friend's own son is marrying a girl from a Jewish Orthodox family.

As means of an explanation, Sally admits that she has blocked out many of the stories from the Holocaust that were told to her by her parents. Her friend, on the other hand, remembers her own parents' trials and tribulations in detail and feels it's an important part of her life as well.

But her friend's devout faith was not always so strong. Prior to her husband's passing, her friend made a pact with G-d that if he cures him, she would only eat Kosher food. In spite of her prayers, her husband did pass away but she kept her promise and turned more toward her Jewish religion. She kept Kosher, went to temple regularly, and as a result of her faith, her children became more religious as well.

"I understand my friend's beliefs, but I believe that religion is in your heart," explains Sally. "I don't think the food we eat or staying home on Saturday is what encompasses religion."

Sally and her family do attend temple, but only on High Holidays, the most holy of the Jewish holidays. For her, like many people who attend church on Sundays, going to temple is an opportunity to connect with others socially. And, as for her sons' girlfriends, she says, "Jewish or not, I adore them."

When her first husband passed away 13 years ago, she admits that she strayed slightly away from the temple, preferring as she said to find religion in her heart. She maintains contact as do her children, but not nearly to the extent of her brother, Lenny, who held an office on his temple's governing board and whose children consider themselves to be "religious."

Today, when Jews struggle with maintaining a remembrance of the Holocaust and wondering if going to temple is the only way to be "Jewish enough" and honor the passing of their relatives, perhaps they can turn to the writing of the Dalai Lama, who created the following passage in September, 2010:

> "My true religion, my simple faith is in love and compassion. There is no need for complicated philosophy, doctrine, or dogma. Our own heart, our own mind, is the temple. The doctrine is compassion. Love for others and respect for their rights and dignity, no matter who or what they are - these are ultimately all we need."

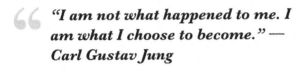

Chapter 7

"I am not what happened to me. I am what I choose to become." — **Carl Gustav Jung**

The Holocaust survivors' suffering did not end with their liberation. Their experience has remained long after World War II ended. Similar to members of military who experience PTSD (post traumatic stress disorder) after they serve, Holocaust survivors also have a form of PTSD. With the click of a few keyboard buttons, one finds nearly 900,000 articles on PTSD symptoms in Holocaust survivors. Their symptoms are real and not only affect them, but their children as well.

In fact, some studies report that now third generations also show signs of stress and anxiety that manifested with their grandparents and the treatment that their parents experienced growing up as a child of a Holocaust survivor.

The effects of trauma on the human psyche varies

with each person and in some, manifests as PTSD and in others, severe psychosis. According to a study by doctors Yoram Barak and Henry Szor of The Psychogeriatric Department, Abarbanel Mental Health Center, Bat Yam, and the Sackler Faculty of Medicine, Tel Aviv University in Israel, 50 years after the Holocaust, the majority of survivors and World War II veterans continue to count their experiences as the "most significant stressors" of their lives.

⁂

LISA LIVES IN ST. LOUIS AND ALTHOUGH SHE describes her mother as loving, she grew up harboring feelings of anger. She resented not having grandparents. She felt humiliated when friends would come over and if the play became too noisy, her mother would complain because she was not familiar with play having spent her young years in a concentration camp. But mainly, Lisa resented being the child of a Holocaust survivor for the emotional issues it propelled onto her.

At age ten, Lisa wanted to attend summer camp with her friends. Her mother denied her, but allowed her older sister to go. Lisa complained, "My sister can go to camp and my parents went to camp. Why can't I go?" She had no understanding at the time of what her mother's "camp" entailed, and when she was older and her mother offered to talk about it, Lisa didn't want to know for fear of hearing the details.

Mainly, Lisa craved normalcy. Her parents' strong accents were another area of embarrassment and she was aware that her mother was different from the "cool and hip" moms. Although her mother didn't fit in, her father began meeting with other survivors to discuss and purchase stocks and property. He became successful in this pursuit.

When Lisa had children of her own, the legacy of the Holocaust sadly continued as her mother felt ill-equipped to take on a grandmotherly role. Lisa was painfully aware that her mother had been fairly absent from her life and now had done the same to her children's lives. She strives to give her own children a happy upbringing.

SALLY REPORTED ANOTHER STORY FROM HER FATHER'S experience in the Holocaust. While in the concentration camp, he heard a noise that came from underneath the soil. To his horror, it was a man buried alive.

Without concern for his own safety, he saved the man. They remained lifelong friends after they left the camp. Sally later became friends with Sharon, the daughter of the man who was saved. And in turn, Sally and Sharon's children became friends.

In a strange occurrence of fate, Sally's son, Ryan, and Sharon's daughter, Lauren, came to know each other without ever realizing their parents' and grandparents' connection. Sharon expressed that the connectivity of being a child to a Holocaust survivor has occurred amongst other friends as well.

ACADEMIC WRITING ON THE SURVIVOR'S MINDSET

One woman confided to Sally that she can't fall asleep without a nightlight and the television remaining on because she is afraid of ghosts. The ghosts she refers to are the Holocaust victims. The stories of them are vivid in her mind from when her parents recalled incidents prior to her going to bed. Why a parent would do this is explained in the academic writing of Dr. Barak and Dr. Szor.

Their paper explains that PTSD persists into old age among survivors. The severity among each person can vary based on their age at the time when they were in concentration camps. Their association with early trauma often leads to chronic and debilitating disease. Some are able to develop coping skills, but often "coping" means not talking about their experience as was the case with Sally's father.

The dramatic variance between not talking about the concentration camp experience and in contrast, retelling stories to a child prior to bedtime, manifests itself in those adult children in far different scenarios. The woman who was told detailed stories about the atrocities of the war believes ghosts visit and are still with her today. The only way she finds peace is an OCD (obsessive compulsive disorder) method of placing a prayer book in the room.

Terror experienced by parents from the Holocaust can be passed down several generations. Depression, schizophrenia, and development of late-life paranoia have all been reported in aging Holocaust survivors. Second generations are even more likely to commit suicide.

In an article titled, "The Effects of the Holocaust on the Children of Survivors," author Lisa Katz reports: "Some survivors did not talk to their children about their Holocaust experiences. These Second Gens were raised in homes of hidden mystery. This silence contributed to a culture of repression within these families. Other survivors talked a great deal to their children about their Holocaust experiences. In some cases, the talk was too much, too soon, or too often."

Katz goes on to describe four primary symptoms of PTSD. These include:

1. Re-experiencing trauma through flashbacks, nightmares, memories, or exaggerated emotional and physical reactions;
2. Emotional numbing;
3. Avoiding situations reminiscent to the trauma; and,
4. Increased arousal such as irritability, hyper-vigilance, exaggerated startle response, and difficulty sleeping.

True PTSD requires that all four symptoms are present. Sadly, for another woman we interviewed for this book, this is exactly what she experiences. Her story is as follows:

Rebecca was raised in a fairly Jewish populated suburb of Detroit, and her upbringing was not unlike many of her friends. Her grandparents were survivors of the Holocaust as were many older people in the neighborhood.

Her grandparents would show her books about the Holocaust. They shared photos of the camps and barracks as well as the Jewish prisoners who were not much more than skin and bones, wearing little to no clothing. The photos were shocking to Rebecca were her grandparents' suffering. Sometimes, they would remove their dentures to show Rebecca how they lost their teeth due to the conditions of living in the camps for five years.

Rebecca's grandmother confided that her younger sister and cousin also survived, but upwards of 50 people in her family, originally from Poland, were murdered.

In 1939, the Germans invaded Poland and more than 400,000 Jews living in Warsaw, the capital city, were confined to an area that was only slightly more than one square mile. Rebecca's brother left the "Warsaw Ghetto" one day to buy bread, but never returned home. Her father went looking for him and was murdered in the street.

Her grandmother's survival was the result of quick thinking. She snuck out of their apartment and traded fabric for food with the gentiles (non-Jews) who she trusted to not report her. The fabrics came from a textiles and clothing factory the family owned.

These relayed stories affected Rebecca throughout her adult life. She suffered severe PTSD characterized by depression and suicidal behavior. Long after the war ended and Rebecca had children of her own, she still experienced night terrors. If her children ever complained about not having nicer clothing or objects, she resorted to talks about Hitler and his return. These scare tactics were not out of malice. In fact, she was proud of her four children, 14 grandchildren and great-grandchildren. She simply could not escape the terrors of the stories that were passed onto her. This defined her until she passed away in 1999 from breast cancer.

❦

TO SPEAK OR TO STAY SILENT

Other survivors made the choice to not speak about their war experience with their children. However, this did not save their children from experiencing the difficulties of being raised by parents who had been sent to the concentration camps.

Originally from Poland, Trisha's parents never spoke of their teen years spent in concentration camps at Bergen Belsen, Aushwitz, and Dachau. They met in the camps and fell in love. After the war, her mother, Esther, contracted tuberculosis and went to Sweden. Her father, Ben, found his love and they married in a Catholic church in Sweden with the ceremony conducted by a rabbi. Although each had many siblings, it was a small, intimate ceremony as they were the only survivors from their respective families.

Ben and Esther had two children, both born in Sweden. They had friends in the United States, who sponsored them for visas and they readily decided to move. However, due to the tuberculosis, Esther wasn't cleared by immigration to come to the U.S. so her friend provided her with her own x-rays to allow Esther's entrance into the United States.

They settled in Minnesota with their two children. Trisha was born shortly after in 1955. As Trisha reached school age, she became aware of differences between her parents and other children's. Trisha's mother only spoke Yiddish, and as a result, never attended any of Trisha's school events or took part in the PTA.

Her mother developed chronic depression and was eventually institutionalized. With no ability to converse in English, she had no friends and felt like an outcast. Feeling ostracized also developed from her mother not dressing like others, nor having her hair styled. She never fit into society in the United States and received little help in this area from her husband.

In fact, Trisha's father often beat her mother along with herself and her younger sister. Although they tried to help their mother, they were not allowed to do housework because their father considered that to be their mother's role. But their mother wasn't fit to maintain a household. She began to suffer from hallucinations and flashbacks.

Trisha's father developed additional problems beyond his rage. He started having heart attacks in his 30s. Because of the rarity to have a heart attack at such a young age, Trisha's sister, Rachel, began to research their father's background in the concentration camps using his tattooed number as a reference point. She learned that he was used for medical experiments and perhaps this was the underlying reason why he began having heart attacks at a young age.

The knowledge that he had undergone something so horrific that it could still wield health issues, gave Trisha and her younger sister, Rachel, tremendous stress. Their parents never spoke of what they had endured. Instead of being saved from pain or fear, the children's imaginations manifested gruesome stories as they wondered what their parents may have undergone.

The children could never speak to their parents about their past as the questions would send their father into a rage. Eventually, he would make up stories to appease the children, but his tales did little to bring them comfort. Rather, they discovered lies and made up stories. Their father had a scar and his explanation of how he received it was that he had been aboard a ship that had been bombed. Yet, the girls knew this was unlikely as he never learned to swim and surely would have perished.

The stressful living conditions affected everyone. Half-truths and lies defined their parents' discussions about the concentration camps. Rage manifested itself into regular beatings starting when Trisha was merely seven-years-old.

Trisha recalls, "My parents were merely shells of a physical body. They showed no emotion, and certainly no love. They exhibited as much rage as if the war was still occurring."

The only one in the family who escaped their father's beatings was Trisha's older sister because she received straight As in school. But Trisha's performance both in school and socially disappointed her father. Poor grades resulted in beatings. When he saw her kiss a Black man, a beating ensued.

Trisha coped by repeatedly running away from home. When Trisha would leave, she would run to her friend, Amelia's, house. Amelia's parents were very loving, but as Holocaust survivors, they too had problems with anxiety. The cycle continued within Amelia, who passed on the trait of anxiety to her two children.

Although she found some respite within Amelia's home, problems still existed and Trisha found she needed to return to her own home. Each time she returned, her dad whipped her with a belt. She never received comfort from her mother because she was also being beaten. By the time she entered high school, Trisha started hitting back.

The abuse not only affected Trisha and her sisters while at home, but also when they sought out relationships of their own. Trisha's older sister's first husband was physically abusive. Her younger sister was not able to form serious relationships. In her 20s, Trisha decided she was a lesbian having never felt an emotional connection to men, fearful of getting too close. Her younger sister made the same choice, but realized her sexual orientation at a younger age.

Trisha married another woman, Amy, when she was in her 30s. Destined to repeat the cycle of abuse, she discovered her wife was a bully. When her wife became abusive, Trisha would cower and remember the years with her father.

Even so, she and Amy had two children, a son and a daughter, through surrogacy. However, growing up in the shadow of her mother's mental incapacity plagued her. Trisha struggled with depression, and when her son left for college, she slept in his room with the door locked. After a lengthy marriage, she and Amy finally divorced.

When their father died at age 61 in the 1980s, Trisha was 28. Trisha grew up believing that you don't have to be a blood relative to be family. Because she had no other family, the people who had sponsored her parents for citizenship were the ones to offer comfort and love.

Professionally, she entered the field of social work to help patients with HIV and AIDS. She made it her mission in life to understand death because it was never spoken about in her family.

At 65, she has undergone therapy and is happy with herself and lives in San Francisco. Her children are grown. Both are heterosexual and her daughter was recently married. One lives in Los Angeles and the other in New York. Trisha wants no contact with her former wife, Amy, and says that she too feels like a survivor.

For some Holocaust survivors, memory is a lifelong burden that they pass onto their children.

However, while trauma can be levied upon new

generations, so can positive traits such as adaptability and resilience. Some families have unfortunately manifested the trauma, but others have learned to cope and adapt to challenges. Family values is a trait that is also passed on from Holocaust survivors and is a characteristic that we hope transcends the trauma.

Chapter 8

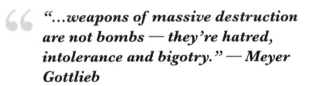

> **"...weapons of massive destruction are not bombs — they're hatred, intolerance and bigotry." — Meyer Gottlieb**

How do children of Holocaust survivors move forward? Perhaps more important, how do we prevent the cycle of mental anguish and disease from affecting future generations?

Most Jews agree that it is important to showcase our cultural and religious history. This includes sharing dances, songs, and food, but also the significance of our Jewish holidays and sadly, the remembrance of Jewish persecution in the Holocaust.

What steps can children of Holocaust survivors take with future generations? How do we continue to share the importance of our relatives' history, but discontinue the psychological disorders that have erupted as a result of these living narratives?

The answers and suggestions that we present come

from a variety of sources including our interviewees, academic papers, the USC Shoah Foundation, founded by director Steven Spielberg, and numerous other organizations dedicated to Holocaust remembrance, education, and support.

NEW MOVEMENTS — HEIGHTENED AWARENESS

Remembering the Holocaust is necessary in order to uphold the values of democracy in today's world.

The Shoah Foundation

The Shoah Foundation's mission is to develop empathy, understanding, and respect through testimony. Founded by Steven Spielberg in 1994, its efforts focus on conducting interviews with survivors and other witnesses of the Holocaust, and preserving these testimonies. It is also referred to as The Institute for Visual History and Education. The Institute houses nearly 55,000 audio-visual testimonies conducted in 65 countries and in 43 languages.

Testimonies of the survivors offer personal history before, during, and after their firsthand experience with genocide. There have been 115,000 hours of video testimony recorded with all content indexed and searchable to the minute.

The Holocaust and the United Nations Outreach Programme

The General Assembly of the United Nations adopted two resolutions relating to the Holocaust. The first, Resolution A/RES/60/7, was adopted on November 1, 2005 and calls for a remembrance of past crimes with an eye towards preventing them in the future. Then, in 2007, the Resolution 61/255 was adopted, which condemns any denial of the Holocaust and urges Member States to reject any similar denial.

International Holocaust Remembrance Day

UNESCO (United Nations Education, Scientific and Cultural Organization) pays tribute to the memory of the victims of the Holocaust and reaffirms its unwavering commitment to counter antisemitism, racism, and other forms of intolerance that may lead to group-targeted violence.

The "Holocaust Remembrance" resolution designates January 27th — the anniversary of the liberation of the Auschwitz death camp — as an annual International Day of Commemoration in memory of the victims of the Holocaust. This remembrance is observed with ceremonies and activities at the United Nations Headquarters in New York and at UN offices around the world. The first year that ceremonies were held in 2006, over 2,200 people came to the UN General Assembly Hall and countless others viewed the proceedings globally via webcast and live television broadcast.

The UNESCO website reminds, "Member States share a collective responsibility for addressing the residual trauma, maintaining effective remembrance policies, caring for historic sites, and promoting education, documentation and research, seven decades after the genocide. This responsibility entails educating about the causes, consequences and dynamics of such crimes so as to strengthen the resilience of young people against ideologies of hatred."

#WeRemember

#WeRemember, the campaign for International Holocaust Remembrance Day, has been widely promoted by The World Jewish Congress (WJC) and UNESCO. Additionally, together the organizations established www.aboutholocaust.org with the goal of providing young people with essential information about the history of the Holocaust and its legacy.

It is an interactive, online tool to provide facts for students, video testimonies of survivors, and the news updates about Holocaust educational programs and activities. Its primary purpose in providing this content is to address misinformation that circulates across social media and other internet forums.

WHERE DO WE GO FROM HERE?

Sally's answer is both simple and poignant: Judaism is in your heart. She adds, "When I see antisemitism I get angry. In the aftermath of George Floyd's death, anger was all around."

Peaceful protests turned violent, fires and looting broke out, and police attempted to disperse crowds with rubber bullets and tear gas. In the midst of the upheaval, a temple in Los Angeles was vandalized.

"They had written 'Fuck Israel' on the outside walls, and it hurt more than I thought it would," says Sally. "The temple started and grew from Holocaust survivors and to see this disregard was painful."

But like true survivors, the congregation didn't let this act deter or break them. They gathered the following morning at 7 a.m. to clean up. "It was heart-warming to see the gathering of different generations in support and solidarity," adds Sally.

She believes knowledge is key to moving forward. At the time of this writing, the #BlackLivesMatter movement has become a global phenomenon. A June 18, 2020 article posted on CNN.com highlighted results from a poll showing undeniable support of the movement over police brutality and discrimination.

The article reports, "A Kaiser Family Foundation poll out Thursday found 64% of Americans supported the recent protests against police violence, including 86% of Democrats, 67% of independents and 36% of Republicans. Support for the protests is seen across racial lines, with 84% of blacks, 64% of Hispanics and 61% of whites in support."

A Pew Research Center poll found similar results. According to their website: "Two-thirds of U.S. adults say they support the movement, with 38% saying they strongly support it. This sentiment is particularly strong among black Americans, although majorities of white (60%), Hispanic (77%) and Asian (75%) Americans express at least some support."

What does this mean for Jews and survivors of the Holocaust? As the public takes steps to educate themselves about racial injustice and inequality, the majority of people recognize that a lack of education is a root cause of racism. The same can be said for antisemitism.

Sally is proud that her children recognize this fact. "My kids won't put up with any type of antisemitism. They know about their grandparents' history. The stories that my mother conveyed stay with them more so than with me because I built up a wall of protection that doesn't let these stories penetrate. My kids may not be

Orthodox, but religious practices are not a gauge of one's affiliation with Judaism. Antisemitism cannot happen."

Sally recalls a time when her son was 12-years-old and a classmate left a message on their answering machine in which he claimed to be a Nazi and wanted to kill the family. Sally promptly called the school, but admits that not much was done. She hopes that the lack of action would not happen today, a few decades later.

Her brother, Lenny, agrees that education is key. "There seems to be an unfounded negativity toward Jewish people, but it's not true antisemitism. It's ignorance."

In terms of #BlackLivesMatter (#BLM), a lot of good was done via social media. But Lenny has seen examples of that not always being the case where people have made light of the Holocaust. He refers to a social media post in which teen girls in Pennsylvania posed with swastika temporary tattoos on their shoulders.

"I'm sure those girls have no intention of rounding up people and throwing them into concentration camps. They just think they're cool rebels. The problem is that it snowballs and others imitate what they see."

Sally questions whether the Covid-19 pandemic, causing people to isolate and spend much more time in their homes, contributed to the power behind #BLM. "There is a strong desire to do something important now. We feel our immortality."

Lenny adds, "During the Holocaust, people were killed for the simple reason of being Jewish. When you talk about an oppressed community, Jewish people are probably the most oppressed people over time; and yet, also the most successful. It's hard to argue that they are discriminated against when so many are doing well for themselves."

Education is in part showing people that what they see is not necessarily true. It's a difficult balance. Lenny recalls a popular sit-com called "Hogan's Heroes." The show aired six seasons on the CBS network from September 17, 1965, to April 4, 1971, the longest broadcast run for an American television series inspired by World War II. The show was set in a German prisoner of war (POW) camp, which Lenny says was a big reason for its acceptance. "It wasn't a concentration camp, which was very different."

Another important distinction was that in the show, the Nazis always appeared bumbling and inept. "If you dilute something you take away the pain from it," explains Lenny. "You start to rationalize more extreme things. Until you get to today where teens wear swastika tattoos."

ARE WE "HARD-WIRED TO BE RACIST"?

Sally didn't miss a beat when she decided to call her son's school after receiving that disturbing voicemail message. Lenny views a social media post showing swastika bearing teens with distaste. And yet, neither believe that one should respond to every incidence of anti-semitism, even in spite of their family history.

"Humans are hard-wired to be racist," claims Lenny. "If you put a family in a locked room and create a dangerous situation, they will protect each other at all costs."

He describes a scenario dating back to when we had tribal societies. If a new tribe approached and was unrecognized, everyone would be apprehensive because of the unfamiliarity... their differences. With the development of transportation, people mingled and started looking less alike. We now have a society with representatives from all over the world living closer. We don't compete for resources and we don't have the same anthropologic need as in tribal times, but we still have that hardwire.

"There will always be someone who says the Jews run the press. But truth be told, it probably is close to the truth because a large portion are Jews and people look at that as a problem. I would joke and say that's a good thing," says Lenny.

COULD THERE BE HISTORICAL IMPLICATIONS FOR ANTISEMITISM?

During the Inquisition, Jews could not own property, but they could get ahead by being money handlers. People didn't view the job of running the bank as positive, but the Jews took it on and did well with it. When people had to flee, they couldn't take an entire house of contents, but they could take gold. This presents a historic context as to why Jewish people frequently are involved in the field of finance. Some say Christopher Columbus was Jewish. His trip to India left on August 2, 1492 — the same day the Jews were forced out of Spain. Additional circumstantial evidence shows he was Jewish and most of his crew were escaping prisoners.

The aspect of handling banking, which was originally seen as a menial task and then became valuable, places into context why Jews were thought of a certain way and how envy comes into play. In fact, envy is probably the biggest contributor to antisemitism. This is a substantial difference between antisemitism toward Jews and racism toward Blacks.

Culture also starts to play a role in antisemitism. Education is a strong component in Jewish upbringing. Rather than focus on sports prowess, many Jewish parents encouraged studying. Perhaps genetics play a role because many Jews met during the Holocaust, married afterwards, and their smaller frame resulted in children that didn't grow up to become the biggest or strongest. Many jokes have been made about children of Jewish households predetermined to grow up to become doctors or lawyers. The ridiculousness of a mother dropping her child off to pre-school with the expectation that it is the first step in their journey toward the pursuit of one of these professions has been told.

In this day of heightened awareness toward becoming an "anti-racist" — to not generalize a person based on their race — we have learned that even if the generalization appears to be complimentary, such jokes demonstrate a form of racism or in the case of the doctor and lawyer, antisemitism.

Lenny and Sally recall their upbringing and the lack of diversity among their parents' friend circle. When Sally's son graduated from New York University, a party was held at Sally's home for family and friends. His grandmother asked, "Who invited all of the Schvartzes?" It's a Yiddish word referring to a Black person. "We knew that in our grandmother's mind, the term was a description much like referring to 'the blonde next door' and yet, we also had enough knowledge to not teach our own children to use such a term," says Sally.

Lenny says, "We all have prejudices. What defines us

is what we do with it. Our actions create issues of racism and antisemitism."

Both Sally and Lenny agree that growing up Jewish, one will hear certain comments. Jews are good with money. Jews are tight with money. Jews are smart. Jews are short. These comments fall under the range of antisemitism, but if the comment is made without malice should one address it?

"You risk becoming a reactionary and crying wolf if you make a big deal out of every comment," says Lenny. "You have to make it count and pick your battles. One needs to realize the world is not perfect. George Washington was a slave owner, but he also did a lot of good. One needs to consider the social context of the day."

HOLLYWOOD'S JEWISH HERITAGE

Jewish citizens, particularly those in the public eye, have a responsibility to bring attention to the Jewish heritage rather than shy away from it. As we have demonstrated, antisemitism continues due to lack of education. With antisemitism comes mistreatment. And, with mistreatment, damaging effects are carried over from the victim to future generations.

Winona Ryder is one actress who admitted that she didn't readily bring attention to her Jewish roots. Perhaps her behavior to keep her religion and culture quiet is our modern equivalent of Jews needing to hide. In Hollywood, she experienced antisemitism, lack of roles, and openly being told she looked "too Jewish." But with more recent successes, she opened up about the legacy of Holocaust trauma in her family.

Like many of the children of Holocaust survivors interviewed for this project, Ryder says she grew up fearful of Nazis lurking. She often slept in the doorway to her parents' bedroom, afraid they may be taken from her and killed. She had learned that her mother's father died fighting Nazis in the Pacific and family members on her father's side died in concentration camps.

On the 70th anniversary of the end of the Holocaust, *The Hollywood Reporter* did its part to commemorate the end of the war and its survivors with emotionally revealing interviews with 11 famous survivors. Titled "The Last Survivors," the publication devoted its cover to the cause on December 16, 2015.

In keeping with the mission of the USC Shoah Foundation, its founder Steven Spielberg, wrote an essay for the feature. Here, we encapsulate each subject's testimony.

ROMAN POLANSKI, DIRECTOR OF "ROSEMARY'S BABY," "Chinatown" and "The Pianist," has been hesitant to speak to the U.S. press for years due to the risk of extradition from Europe, but for this purpose, which he deemed vitally important, he spoke to Peter Flax, an editor at *The Hollywood Reporter*, about his Holocaust experience.

Polanski saw a woman killed before his eyes. He described her blood flowing "like a fountain." He also spoke to Flax about his interview for the Shoah Foundation, a five-hour testimony, which shows Polanski walking through his native Krakow, Poland.

Flax wrote, "He points out the spot where he slipped through barbed wire to escape the ghetto, tours the first ghetto apartment his family called home and muses about how opposite sides of a city street could demarcate life and death."

🌿

Branko Lustig, Academy Award-winning producer of "Schindler's List" and "Gladiator," was a prisoner at age 12 when the British army liberated Auschwitz. He recalls thinking that he had finally died when he heard the army's bagpipes playing, believing it was the sound of angels' music.

He met Spielberg years later while the director was developing "Schindler's List." The commemorative issue of *The Hollywood Reporter* quoted Lustig's description of the encounter: "He kissed my number [from the concentration camp, tattooed on Lustig's arm] and said, 'You will be my producer.' He is the man who gave me the possibility to fulfill my obligation," Lustig says.

🌿

Meyer Gottlieb, president of Samuel Goldwyn Films and producer of "Master and Commander," "The Secret Life of Walter Mitty" and "Tortilla Soup," left Poland as a child in the early 1940s. Most of his relatives were forced to dig their own graves and the knowledge of this horrific fate made Gottlieb decide now to return to his native village. It wasn't until 2008, six decades later, that he finally returned.

He poignantly told *The Hollywood Reporter*: "The truth of the matter is that the weapons of massive destruction are not bombs — they're hatred, intolerance and bigotry."

※

ROBERT CLARY, ONE OF THE ACTORS FROM "HOGAN'S Heroes," the sit-com set in a German POW camp that this book has mentioned previously, sang alongside an accordionist for German soldiers. He believes his joie de vivre and energy kept him alive in the Buchenwald concentration camp as a child.

He later reported: "Singing, entertaining and being in good health at my age, that's why I survived," he says. "I was very immature and young and not fully realizing what situation I was involved with; I don't know if I would have survived if I really knew that."

※

LEON PROCHNIK, WHO ADAPTED THE PLAY, "CHILD'S Play," into a screenplay later directed for film by Sidney Lumet, was the son of a Jewish chocolate factory owner in Krakow. As a child, he believed the tub containing melted chocolate had magical powers. He retold stories of "great things" that happened following his visits to the factory to steal chocolate.

Among these great moments was the time when his father connected with diplomat Chiune Sugihara, who later became known as the "Japanese Schindler" and helped thousands of Jews leave Europe. In another incident, a Jewish prayer book was in the factory, but a Nazi officer conducting a search missed it.

DR. RUTH WESTHEIMER, LEGENDARY SEX THERAPIST
and television/radio personality, never saw her parents
after she turned 10. At 17, she moved to British-
controlled Palestine and trained as a sniper in the
Haganah, a precursor to the Israel Defense Forces.

She told an audience in Tel Aviv and later recalled
for *The Hollywood Reporter*, "Looking at my four grandchildren, Hitler lost and I won."

CURT LOWENS, WHOSE NAME WAS ORIGINALLY
Loewenstein, escaped Berlin and assumed his new iden-
tity in Holland. There, he joined a three-person Dutch
resistance cell and proceeded to save 123 Jewish children
by getting them to safety with Dutch families who agreed
to hide them. After V-E Day, Lowens received a commen-
dation from Gen. Dwight D. Eisenhower for also rescuing
two American airmen.

Known for his acting on film and stage, he portrayed
many Nazi characters including Dr. Josef Mengele in the
Broadway play "The Deputy".

BILL HARVEY MANAGED TO MAINTAIN A POSITIVE
outlook on life in spite of the tragedies he witnessed at
just 21-years-old while in the concentration camps. He
was transported from Auschwitz to Buchenwald on a
frigid cattle car, where he fell unconscious due to
weighing just slightly more than 70 pounds. He was

believed to be dead and piled on top of other corpses awaiting to be cremated.

Someone pulled him from the pile and miraculously he survived and later became a Hollywood cosmetologist to the likes of Judy Garland, Mary Martin, Zsa Zsa Gabor, and Liza Minelli.

He told *The Hollywood Reporter*: "My humble explanation for all the tragedies and the bad people who want just to kill is that maybe there have to be some bad things in order to appreciate all the good things that this world gives you."

⚘

RUTH POSNER WAS A NATURAL BORN ACTRESS, perhaps out of necessity. While living in the Warsaw Ghetto, she and her aunt surreptitiously crossed to the Aryan side of the street, removed and hid their yellow armbands and assumed new identities. She managed to escape the fate of many Jews and kept the story a secret for decades.

She became the founding member of the London Contemporary Dance Company and an actress in the Royal Shakespeare Company. In recalling her story of escape, she told *The Hollywood Reporter*, "Now when I talk about it, it seems like I'm describing my role in a play."

⚘

DARIO GABBAI, WAS AN ACTOR IN THE 1953 WAR film "The Glory Brigade". During the Holocaust, he was sent to the Auschwitz concentration camp and tasked with being a member of the Sonderkommando, prisoners who were forced, or threatened with death themselves, to aid with the disposal of gas chamber victims.

In an interview, he recalled seeing two of his friends from his native Thessaloniki, Greece, in line outside a gas chamber. He said to *The Hollywood Reporter*, "I have inside some stuff I can never tell. I saw so many things. Even now, I like to cry to get it out of my system. But it doesn't go out."

At the time of this writing, Gabbai is thought to be the last living member of the Sonderkommando. Despite the better conditions in which this group lived, most became increasingly weak from the camp condition and were killed as well. Others, whose health endured, were also killed as the Nazis wanted to hide evidence and witnesses of their horrific acts.

❦

AMELIA BINIAZ, WHOSE TESTIMONY WAS INCLUDED in the DVD version of "Schindler's List" was on the historic list of Jews saved by Oskar Schindler. She relayed a story when production was beginning on the film. Some members of the production team believed that actor Liam Neeson was "too handsome" to be cast in the role. She answered, "I told them that Mr. Schindler was very handsome, so he gets the job."

❦

MOVING FORWARD

Years ago, people would lament that they couldn't change the world. In all fairness, it can seem overwhelming for one individual to speak up against injustice or to raise their hand in support of another. Yet, as social media campaigns and hashtags spread and grow, we have proof that one person can speak up and have their voice joined by others. Suddenly, one post or one tweet becomes an international movement.

Speak up against injustice, but plan your actions and words. Make your words count. While random acts of kindness are recognized, random acts of strength are not always heard. Change does not occur overnight, but we have the best chance of making a change when we act as one.

Unify your actions. Support organizations such as those mentioned in this book that are already in the trenches to eradicate antisemitism. And remember, injustice against one group of people makes it acceptable to do harm to other groups. Practice kindness and tolerance for all.

From the United Nations official website:

> *"Recalling the Universal Declaration of Human Rights, the United Nations General Assembly reaffirms that the Holocaust, which resulted in the murder of one-third of the Jewish people along with countless members of other minorities, will forever be a warning to all people of the dangers of hatred, bigotry, racism and prejudice."*

Bibliography

Books

Wiesel, Elie. *Night*. Hill & Wang, 1960. Bantam Books, 1982.

Online Resources

2017 Women's March
  https://en.wikipedia.org/wiki/

Barak, Yoram, MD, and Szor, Henry, MD. "Lifelong post traumatic stress disorder: evidence from aging Holocaust survivors." Dialogues in Clinical Neuroscience. March, 2000.
  https://www.ncbi.nlm.nih.gov/pmc/
articles/PMC3181591/

Botelho, Greg, and Yan, Holly. CNN.com, "George Zimmerman Found Not Guilty of Murder in Trayvon Martin's Death". Sun July 14, 2013

https://www.cnn.com/2013/07/13/justice/
zimmerman-trial/index.html

Callimachi, Rukmini. *Freed From ISIS, Yazidi Women Return in 'Severe Shock'.* New York Times, July 27, 2017.

The Economist. *Archivists are racing to identify every Jewish Holocaust victim.* January 25, 2020. https://www.economist.com/graphic-detail/2020/01/25/archivists-are-racing-to-identify-every-jewish-holocaust-victim

Genocide Watch. https://www.genocidewatch.com/countries-at-risk

Golden, Jonathan. Sarna, Jonathan D. National Humanities Center. *The American Jewish Experience in the Twentieth Century: Antisemitism and Assimilation.* http://nationalhumanitiescenter.org/tserve/twenty/tkeyinfo/jewishexpb.htm

"International Holocaust Remembrance Day"
https://en.unesco.org/commemorations/holocaustremembranceday

International Holocaust Remembrance Alliance Memo on Spelling of Antisemitism IHRA Committee on Antisemitism and Holocaust Denial
April 2015
https://www.holocaustremembrance.com/sites/default/files/memo-on-spelling-of-antisemitism_final-1.pdf

"The Holocaust and the United Nations Outreach Programme".
https://www.un.org/en/holocaustremembrance/

Katz, Lisa. "The Effects of the Holocaust on the Children of Survivors." ThoughtCo.com, March 7, 2019. https://www.thoughtco.com/holocaust-effects-on-children-of-survivors-2076561

Kerstein, Benjamin. "Actress Winona Ryder Opens Up About Her Family's Holocaust Trauma: 'I'm Grateful My Parents Told Me the Truth'". The Algemeiner, July 12, 2020.
https://www.algemeiner.com/2020/07/12/actress-winona-ryder-opens-up-about-her-familys-holocaust-trauma-im-grateful-my-parents-told-me-the-truth/

Kranz, Michal. 5 *Genocides that are Still Going on Today.* Business Insider. Nov. 22, 2017, 1:59 p.m. https://www.businessinsider.com/genocides-still-going-on-today-bosnia-2017-11

Langer, Armin. Evolve website. "Anti-Semitism or anti-semitism? And why the Hyphen Matters
Hyphenating the word "antisemitism" gives the erroneous impression that Semitism exists—either as an innate ethnic characteristic of all Jews or as an ideology held by all Jews."
http://evolve.reconstructingjudaism.org/antisemitism-hyphen

Library of Congress, Exhibitions. *From Haven to Home: 350 Years of Jewish Life in America*

A Century of Immigration, 1820-1924. https://www.loc.gov/exhibits/haventohome/haven-century.html

McDonell-Parry, Amelia, and Barron, Justine, "Death of Freddie Gray: 5 Things You Didn't Know". Rolling Stone, April 12, 2017.
https://www.rollingstone.com/culture/culture-features/death-of-freddie-gray-5-things-you-didnt-know-129327/

Parker, Kim; Menasce Horowitz, Juliana; Anderson, Monica. "Amid Protests, Majorities Across Racial and Ethnic Groups Express Support for the Black Lives Matter Movement". Pew Research Center. June 12, 2020
https://www.pewsocialtrends.org/2020/06/12/amid-protests-majorities-across-racial-and-ethnic-groups-express-support-for-the-black-lives-matter-movement/

Sales, Ben. "Why does a Google search for 'Jewish baby strollers' yield anti-Semitic images?" The Times of Israel, September 26, 2020.
https://www.timesofisrael.com/why-does-a-google-search-for-jewish-baby-strollers-yield-anti-semitic-images/

Shields, Jacqueline. "Concentration Camps: The Sonderkommando". Jewish Virtual Library, A Project of AICE.
https://www.jewishvirtuallibrary.org/the-sonderkommando

Sitrin, Carly, "Donald Trump Tweeted a very Different Statement about Charlottesville than other Officials".

Vox, August 12, 2017.
https://www.vox.com/2017/8/12/16138666/
donald-trump-tweeted-different-statement-
charlottesville-rally-white-nationalist

Sparks, Grace. "Polls show widespread support of Black Lives Matters protests and varied views on how to reform police." CNN.com, June 18, 2020
https://www.cnn.com/2020/06/18/politics/protests-
polling-support-movement-policies-kaiser-
quinnipiac/index.html

Valdosta State University. *What is History? How do Historians study the past as contrasted with Non-historians?* Valdosta, Georgia. https://www.valdosta.edu/
history/documents/what-is-history.pdf

World Jewish Congress. #WeRemember
https://weremember.worldjewishcongress.org/

Zauzmer, Julie, "We were never taught': Young Jews in the U.S. encounter anti-Semitism Firsthand". The Washington Post, November 4, 2018.
https://www.washingtonpost.com/religion/2018/11/
04/we-were-never-taught-young-jews-us-encounter-anti-
semitism-first-hand/

Made in the USA
Las Vegas, NV
10 March 2021

19324604R00059